Scarborough a History of the Town and its People.

W.M. Rhodes

Also, by W.M. Rhodes

Filey a History of the Town and its People

ISBN:978-0-9957752-06

Dr Pritchard The Poisoning Adulterer.

ISBN:978-0-9957752-4-4

978-0-9957752-6-8

Scarborough a History of the Town and its People Copyright. W.M. Rhodes 2018.

ISBN: 978-09957752 -9-9

ISBN: 978-09957752 -7-5

A copy of this book has been lodged with The British Library. Edited by Maureen Vincent-Northam

Book Design Rhys Vincent-Northam & Beenish Qureshi Printed and bound in the United Kingdom.

Published by La-di Dah Publishing.

Introduction

The inspiration to write this book came from walking on the beach at Scarborough envisaging Mrs Farrer stumbling upon a natural spring of rust coloured water bubbling over rocks. I couldn't help thinking did this respected gentlewoman realise what she had uncovered? Not only did she have the insight to realise the potential of these mineral waters, which professed to cure various ailments from arthritis to a tonic for the mind but was instrumental in claiming Scarborough's place as a fashionable Spa Town, then Britain's first seaside resort.

Scarborough is a quintessential English seaside town steeped in history, yet it is relatively unchanged. The town has everything from its humble beginnings to a Roman signal station, a Castle, Sieges, famous people, miles of golden sands, entertainment, cricket festivals and a wonderful open-air theatre.

Acknowledgements

Countless hours of research have gone into making this book possible, which could not have been completed without the records of historians of Scarborough past and present, who have tirelessly recorded the history of the town, especially Hinderwell, Theakston, Cole, Barker and Rowntree.

A special thanks to the Cayley family, Rotunda Museum, Scarborough Maritime Heritage, Scarborough Facebook groups, and all the lovely people who have given me their permission to reproduce photographs.

Thank you.

Dedication

To Our Grandchildren.

Be Kind Be Happy

Contents

Part One Prehistoric

Thousands of years ago the Yorkshire coastline was different from what we see today. Scarborough's hills such as Castle Hill and Oliver's Mount were under the sea and covered in vast sheets of ice. Over time, the earth's climate changed, temperatures warmed, and the ice retreated, which allowed the hills to rise above sea-level and form the backbone of the town of Scarborough that we know today.

Back then, it was not unusual to see marine reptiles prowling Scarborough's coast. Regular visitors would be the Plesiosaurus, recognisable by its long neck and broad paddle flippers, or the Ichthyosaurus which resembled a prehistoric dolphin with razor type teeth. In the sky, the birdlike Pterodactyl with its bat-like wings and elongated fingers would gaze upon the sea ready to swoop down and pounce on its prey.

Many years later, due to a gradual shift in climate and differing sea levels, these great marine monsters died out. The white Cretaceous cliffs of Flamborough and the chalk Wolds of the East Riding were being built up by minute organisms. Humans began to gather and hunt food and evolved behaviours that helped them respond to the challenges of survival in changeable surroundings.

*

The Mesolithic Age (Middle Stone Age)

With the retreat of the glaciers came a steep rise in sea levels, which first separated Britain from Ireland, then the bridge between mainland Europe was severed, and Britain became an island.

The climate in Britain decreased, and large-bodied animals soon became extinct, quickly followed by growth in the forests and significant redistribution of animals and plants. Subsequently, after the climate stabilised, trees grew, and the woods and lakes brim with food.

People travelled northward into once glaciated areas, laid down roots and adopted new survival methods. As hunters, they developed many ways to gather food and generally targeted medium-bodied animals such as red and roe deer, aurochs, elk, sheep and goat. Marine mammals, fish, and shellfish became the staple diet in coastal areas. The animals which they killed for food also provided them with bone and antlers, from which they could make tools or weapons, and skins, which could be utilised, not only for clothing but also for sacks and water carriers.

Plant resources such as hazelnuts, acorns, and nettles became an essential part of Mesolithic diets. Farming communities began to develop, and humans started their first steps in land management.

Forever resourceful, these people burnt swamps and wetlands and made sharp axes from stone and bones, which they used as tools to cut down trees, and for constructing living quarters and fishing vessels.

These hunter-gathers travelled around the country tracking animal migrations and plant changes, developing permanent and semi-permanent communities on the coast, with smaller temporary hunting camps located further inland.

The Mesolithic period lasted from the end of the Ice Age until the start of the farming. This period witnessed the development of smaller and finer stone tools like spearheads and arrows, which allowed the early hunters to become masters of their environment. They built and used canoes for the first time during this period, which implies that men could hunt and fish.

*

The Neolithic Age

The Neolithic or New Stone Age commenced from the start of the farming which arrived in Britain circa 4000-3500 BC. People settled and villages formed, the needs and diet of these Europeans evolved, hence the need to grow grains and cereals for food. Also, animals like sheep and cows were domesticated widely, providing a ready source of meat, leather, bone and milk.

Grain became one of the first foods to be stored for an extended period, which for the first time led to the people laying down permanent roots. In this period, people developed crafts such as weaving and pottery. Large-scale construction started, and people each took on various roles such as fighter, ruler, priest, farmer and leader.

With a more settled Neolithic lifestyle, the style of the houses they built also changed, walls were added to their buildings, which they made from intertwined hazel and willow rods with a mixture of, straw, dung and clay (previously they lived in tents made from animal skins). Thatched roofs provided a warmer, and wind-proof structure. Earlier houses were mostly rectangular, but around 3,500 BCE they became round. Perhaps such a change coincided with the arrival of circular ritual monuments, such as passage graves and hedges.

*

Star Carr

In 1949, local amateur archaeologist John Moore found a single flint blade lying in a ditch in a field five miles from Scarborough. He returned to this same site a year later and uncovered a dense concentration of early Mesolithic flint confirming the first hint of prehistoric activity. Moore contacted Grahame Clark a lecturer of prehistory at Cambridge University who, together with his team, excavated the site. A Stone Age settlement was discovered, which is possibly the most important Mesolithic site in Europe. (Illustrated London News)

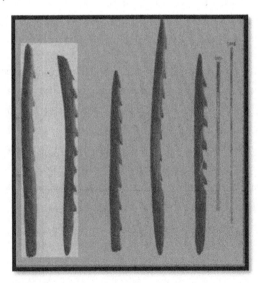

Flint blades probably used for fishing Star Carr 1949. (Illustrated London News)

These significant findings are one of the most important in the archaeological world. One of the team's most interesting finds was a man-made platform possibly a stone-age camping site on what looked like a lakeshore.

Illustrated London News 29/10/1949

On top and within this platform the excavators discovered a range of animal remains red deer, roe deer, wild boar, elk, auroch (wild cow), birds, beaver, pine marten, hedgehog, hare and badger. The relics of a wolf were also excavated, possibly revealing the remains of a domesticated dog. These remains are now in the British Museum.

Further excavations were made to the site in 1985, where a trench was discovered, which revealed the earliest signs of carpentry ever recorded in Europe.

In 2016 the Star Carr archaeology team won the prestigious 'Best Archaeological Innovation Award for their project involving the examination of a unique Mesolithic engraved pendant from Star Carr.' A well-deserved accolade for all involved in the project.

*

Britain's Oldest House

In 2010, archaeologists from the Universities of Manchester and York made a sensational discovery at Star Carr when they excavated 'Britain's oldest house'. This remarkable find revealed that over 11,000 years ago hunter-gatherers occupied this house when Britain was still attached to continental Europe. This excavation reveals that this house is dated 500 years earlier than the previous recorded 'oldest house'.

The house measured 3.5 meters in diameter, with a circle of timber posts around a sunken circular floor area, which could have been covered by reeds. The walls of the house consisted of up to 18 upright posts, each on average around 20 centimetres in diameter. The roof shape couldn't be identified but is believed to be flat, thatched or covered in animal hides. Built sometime between 9200 and 8500 BC, the occupants constructed a living/sleeping area – a 20-30-centimetres-thick layer of moss, reeds and other soft organic material deliberately placed in a shallow 2.5-metre diameter man-made depression. Burnt flints inside the house suggest that the building also had a small hearth.

This incredible site, inhabited after the last ice age, is believed to have been in use for between 200 and 500 years.

*

Falsgrave

Unlike the neighbouring town of Filey, Scarborough is not mentioned in 'the Great Survey of England' known as the Domesday Book compiled in 1086 on the orders of William 1st for defining land ownership and tax obligations. This is most likely because at that time Scarborough was a part of Falsgrave or 'Walesgrif' or 'Walesgrave' which is mentioned in this great book.

Many years ago, Falsgrave was governed by two separate bodies under the old parochial system of self-government and an elected body known as 'The Falsgrave Town Trust'. The latter was elected annually, at a meeting of resident freeholders and ratepayers of the township.

The trust was empowered to manage the Parish lands and other property left or bequeathed, under the provision of the old Enclosure Act for various purposes in the interest of the ratepayers. They had under their care 'The Grammar School' including the appointment of a schoolmaster.

Also, four parcels of land known locally as 'Clay Bank' or 'Mud Field' as it was affectionately known; 'Quarry Bank' which supplied stones for house-building and repairing roads; Fountain or 'Bull Field' was set apart for keeping a Bull, and Oxcliffe and 'Bell Corner' let for agricultural purposes.

The rents derived from the various properties were used for educating a limited number of children, paying a part of the schoolmasters' salary, also the assistant overseers' salary. The rents also went to maintain a village pump and water supply and for other parochial purposes.

With the consent of the Charity Commissioners, these lands were sold in the mid-1800s.

The interest derived from the sale and proceeding investments run by the Scarborough United Scholarships Foundation Trust awarded scholarships of no more than eight pounds a year to both boys and girls age eleven. The sale of the property altogether amounted to five-thousand pounds, which brought in the interest of one-hundred and fifty pounds a year.

Falsgrave had its own pottery situated on 'Clay Field' (Mud Field) which was near to the horse pond; the owners lived close by in a thatched cottage near the schoolhouse. Unfortunately, the pottery did not have a good reputation hence the saying that if something wasn't very good then it was 'like Falsgrave Pottery.'

The Romans

We know that Scarborough is not mentioned in the Domesday Book, therefore it is difficult for us to describe precisely how many settlers there were in Scarborough during this period as no accurate records exist. For centuries, we know little of the history of the first inhabitants of Scarborough.

The Romans had established themselves in Britain, and as enterprising people encouraged architecture, taught their soldiers to build roads, open canals and work mines and how to protect themselves from their enemies.

Law and language were also of great importance as was the obedience of the manners of Rome which the Romans expected to be always respected to protect individuals from the incursion of rapine and plunder. The Romans would not hesitate to 'prosecute' those who went against their laws.

Military roads were constructed to secure the seacoast against ferocious invaders and to communicate between the maritime garrisons and the grand station of York.

In 1922, Mr F.C Simpson excavated a Roman Signal station on Castle Hill, which had been hidden from view, buried beneath the turf of the vast Eastern part of Scarborough Castle's environs. It seems there was a strong tower with 10 feet thick walls, probably rising to around 100 feet. This section continued up to several storey's lit by narrow windows, which would have accommodated the garrison. The flat-top must have been constructed to resist heat if beacon fires were used for signalling purposes. The upper floors were strengthened by pillars on stone bases, which were like the five stones found on Filey Brigg (W.M. Rhodes *History of Filey The Town and its People 2017.*)

Scarborough Signal station and the remains date back from between 360 and 380 BC and consisted of seven bases, and an outer bank and ditch, an enclosure wall and a central tower, which would most likely have housed a beacon. Surrounding the tower was a small courtyard protected by five-feet-thick walls, with flanking turrets at each corner, and a narrow parapet running around it, which could defend against attack.

It is unsure just when the tower fell, but it is thought to have been through fierce combat like the Roman signal station found at Goldsborough near Whitby where several (skeletal) bodies were found thrust down a well in the yard.

*

Furthermore, the Romans formed camps, in the most strategic of places, to prevent the enemy from attacking them. The lofty promontory of Scarborough, on which the castle ruins stand, and the high hills of Weaponess and Oliver's Mount, and Seamer-Moor have provided natural barriers from any unwanted invasion, and the signal stations must have been formidable when occupied by Roman troops.

*

The Anglo Saxons

The Romans ruled England for over four centuries, but by the end of the 5th century it was impossible for them to defend themselves against internal rebellion and external threats and so they were reduced to seeing their Empire subverted by hordes of fierce barbarians. Around the year 446, after five hundred years of rule, they left the British shores.

Britons, deserted by their protectors, lacked the skills to protect themselves from the incursions of the Caledonians, who broke down walls and wasted much of northern Britain. In a moment of despair, they invited over the Saxons, and joining forces they defeated the Caledonians. This decision proved fatal for Britain as the Saxons, allured by the fertile plains of the country, had no desire to return to their land. They reinforced their army, and bent their arms against the natives, with ferocious consequences.

In the year 547, Ida a Saxon Prince with a multitude of men from Germany landed at Flamborough Head and desolated all the neighbouring seacoast. He extended his conquests to the north and conquered what we now know as Northumberland and the south-east of Scotland where he assumed the title of King of Bernicia. Another Saxon Prince named Ælla overcame Lancashire and a considerable part of Yorkshire and took the name of King of Deira. The River Tees was the boundary between these two kingdoms, Bernicia on the north, and Deira on the south.

The Saxon government, laws, manners and language were introduced, and all previous institutions and preferences for art and the culture was abolished, returning to a time of barbarism and slavery. The most important thing to the Saxons was domination and power. The Saxons occupied the Roman foundations in Britain and gave them the appellation of Burgh, which signified that the place homed a family of ten people, but as castles were built to defend the towns, the term Burgh was then known to mean 'a fortified place'. These Burghs were of Royal creation, protected with walls or castles, and inhabited by mechanics, tradesmen and merchants, who enjoyed the privileges of that town.

During the reign of Alfred, the Great, an intelligent and merciful man who encouraged education in England decreed that lessons should be taught in English and not in Latin. He also improved the country's legal system and military structure, therefore improving the quality of life for many Britons. The Saxons were concerned over the invasions of Britain by the Danes, who frequently crossed the German ocean, with numerous fleets, to commit their deprivations on the Eastern coast of Britain. Scarborough, Whitby, and Flamborough Head were the places upon the shore most vulnerable, due to their convenient promontories convenient to landing. Flamborough Head bears the testimony of a Danish encampment, and to this day is still known as Little Denmark.

To stem the tide of desolation King Alfred had to resort to any means, and for a time adopted the men of war and menace, which did nothing to bring peace to the land. Meanwhile, the Danes were joined by swarms from the Baltic who descended on the country and were met with no resistances and subdued the whole country. His friends soon deserted Alfred and drove from his throne. During his exile, Alfred learned that his captures were becoming careless. Eventually, he found the courage to escape and with a group of faithful followers he disguised himself as a Harper and visited a Danish camp. Finally, Alfred and his men won a decisive victory at the battle of Edington in 878.

Alfred knew only too well that his victory would be meaningless unless he followed it up with measures to strengthen the area under his control. Therefore, Burghs, or fortified towns, were set up. Alfred also encouraged settlement of these towns, which acted as a string of border fortresses, armed and held at the ready against possible Danish incursions. This system did much to stabilise the political situation and bring a measure of peace to the once ravaged islands.

On occasions, in the villages surrounding Scarborough Roman antiquities have been found. In 1768 several Roman urns containing bones and ashes were in Staintondale when the hills were excavated for gravel. One of the most significant finds was at Ravenhill Hall was discovered in 1774, when Captain Child's workmen were digging the foundations for the hall and came upon a twenty-two-inch stone at the bottom of some ruins on which is this inscription.

Whitby author Lionel Charlton wrote in 1779 in his book *The History of Whitby* (1779) where he translates this tablet to mean, 'Justinian, the father of his country, the Conqueror of Vandals, Moors, Africans, Samaritans, and Britons, the most excellent Emperor of the Romans, four PrÆtor, built this castle for the use of navigation.'

Possibly, this stone was the foundation stone for a fort or castle, built during the reign of Justinian for protecting the Yorkshire Coast, and by its situation on a promontory would most probably have been a watchtower, or a lighthouse, to direct ships in the proper course for Flamborough Head or Whitby Harbour.

What is exciting about this discovery is that if the translation on the stone is correct, it depicts Roman occupation a century after the Romans departed the British shores. However, it is most likely that the Saxons after obtaining a footing in Britain, readily occupied this Roman station, especially when they saw how strategically well-chosen it was for maritime purposes.

This station most likely stood for many years on the coast until Hungar and Hubba two celebrated Danish chieftains who no doubt destroyed it.

*

In 1857, The Hull Packet reported that Lord Londesborough had found archaeological relics on his land a limestone quarry at Seamer. Twenty years previously, skeletons had been found nearby which were re-interred in St Mary's churchyard. (Hull Packet)

The previously unbroken land was excavated and revealed a beautiful lozenge-shaped pendant of gold, an elegant gold pin, gold fragments believed to be a part of a necklace and a considerable amount of broken pottery. Shards of iron staples and nails were also found indicating that the body of the possessor of these valuable items was encased in a wooden case or coffin. Interestingly, also found was a large piece of glass, understood to be a part of a glass vessel of some magnitude? At the time Lord Londesborough's men were about to excavate more of the area when they came across another coffin containing a skeleton, but no artefacts. This skeleton was in a foetal position with a small knife to one side of the skeleton's left hand; on the right were fragments of iron, possibly from a small purse.

At the time the Scarborough Philosophical and Archaeological Society declared, 'that there can be no doubt that there was an early Anglo Settlement near Scarborough and that it was of great importance and consisted of wealthy families. (Hull Packet, 16/10/1857)

*

The Saxons & The Danes

In the spring of 876, Hungar & Hubba got together a diverse fleet and set sail for England. These men and their crew were barbarians who regardless of sex or age would think nothing of rape and plunder; they would ravage a town, steal all valuables then set the town alight. In 876 the Chieftains landed on the coast of England in two divisions. The first division commanded by Hubba landed at Dunsley Bay (near Whitby) where on a high piece of ground they erected a standard (a raven) this ground has been known ever since as Raven Hill.

Hangar, with the other division, landed at Streonshalh (Robin Hood's Bay) where again, on the top of the cliff, they also erected a standard in a flag with a raven on it, which is still also known as Raven Hill.

*

The Norman Conquest & Scarborough: The Origins of its Name

There are a few different versions of where Scarborough gets its name. The earliest appellation is the name Scaerburg of Saxon origin meaning Scear a rock and burg a fortified place, which leads us to believe that Scarborough is most probably a Saxon town on a Roman foundation.

A mediaeval Icelandic saga tells the story of two Viking brothers Thorgills and Kormack (Cormack) who were the first men to establish the fort called Skarðaborg in the year 966. The fort so-called after Thorgillis whose nickname was Skardi meaning hare-lipped and Borg or Burg meaning fort.

However, the settlement did not last long as it was plundered and burned to the ground by Tostig, Earl of Northumberland the brother of Harold, King of England who had dispossessed Tostig for cruelty.

The Normans

Rolf Ragnvaldsson (a Viking) known as Rolf 'the Ganger' or simply 'Rollo' because of his incredible size sailed to the north of France and conquered the land on either side of the Seine. The King of France was then Charles III whose byname was Charles the Simple, who was not a match for the powerful Viking Warrior.

Rollo's name figured prominently in the treaty between King Charles the Simple and the Seine Vikings in 911. By that eminent agreement, the Vikings received control of the territory at the mouth of the Seine in return for certain services to the King. Rollo himself was granted Upper Normandy (the territory between the Epte River and the sea), and he was converted to Christianity and baptized by the archbishop of Rouen. Rouen was the capital of the ecclesiastical province of Normandy, which Rollo's successors later added to their initial territory.

The offspring of Rollo and his followers became known as the Normans. Rollo is the great-great-great-grandfather of William the Conqueror, or William I of England. Through William, he is one of the ancestors of the present-day British royal family, as well as an ancestor of all current European monarchs and a great many claimants to abolished European thrones.

Edward preferred the Normans to the English and introduced Norman ways and architecture into England. During his reign, he kept up a correspondence with Normandy and when he died, he left his kingdom to William the Duke of Normandy.

In the year 1066, Tostig brother of Harold became Earl of Northumberland, but he was so unpopular he was sent into exile. In revenge for his disgrace, Tostig engaged the services of Haralld Hadrada King of Norway. Together with a multitude of warriors they sailed across the British Ocean and landed at Shetland.

They went a long way around before they reached Scarborough. They had considered that people from the south of England were much more tractable and docile than those from the north, as following the Battle of Hastings, the Normans had little trouble south of the Trent, but in Yorkshire, the rebellion of the people took all William's courage to stop them.

These warriors first made themselves the masters of the rock upon which Scarborough castle now stands, they then heaped together a pile of tree trunks, branches and rubble and set fire to them throwing sizeable burning fire boards down onto the hill engulfing the town below, which was constructed of nothing more than highly combustible wooden huts. The fire quickly spread from one house to another.

Creative Commons Licence

The invaders, having slain great numbers, plundered every article capable of removal and the only terms on which they spared the lives of the conquered people was that they surrender themselves and their families unconditionally to the King. These actions all account for why there is no mention of the town of Scarborough in the Domesday Book of 1086.

Scarborough Castle

Public Domain

William le Gros, 2nd Earl of Holderness, 3rd Earl of Albemarle, and Earl of York, (after 1138) was the most powerful baron of his time in the northern counties of England. At the beginning of King Stephen's reign, William le Gros held the continental county of Albemarle, almost the entire peninsula of Holderness, and considerable estates in Lincolnshire. King Stephen gave William great responsibilities and power in Yorkshire after he won the battle of the Standard (Battle of Northallerton) against King David of Scotland, where he earned the title 'The Earl of Yorkshire'. William represented the king on the panel that chose the Archbishop of York, was given charge of the royal forests of

Yorkshire and was given the administrative power of the sheriff of Yorkshire.

William built a castle on the headland above Scarborough in a similar strategic position to that of the Roman signal station centuries earlier. The possession of this vital fortress must have added to the power and influence of William le Gros, an irreplaceable warrior in the King's eyes. However, on the ascension of Henry II; he experienced sheer humiliation when the King reduced the extreme power of the nobles and commanded that all castles built during the reign of the previous king should be demolished. King Henry embarked north on ensuring that his orders were carried out, but Scarborough Castle with its dangerous position became too great a defence to the seacoast, so the king preserved it. However, he ordered it to be rebuilt and strengthened to fortify a more magnificent structure.

The Earl of Albemarle resented the loss of his castle, which had cost him considerable time and money to build. To revenge the injury, he fortified himself in Bytham Castle Lincolnshire and kept all the neighbouring county in subjection.

The Earl was summoned before the court, but instead of proceeding to London he travelled north to Northampton and seized Fotheringhay Castle where he secured it with a strong garrison – he later returned to Bytham for refuge. However, on hearing the march of the Kings Army, he withdrew to the north and with assistance from The Archbishop of York he obtained a pardon.

William le Gros was so affected by his reverse of fortune that in 1179 he retired from public life to a sequestered retreat in Lincolnshire where he died.

*

Black Dog Knight

The Head of Piers de Gavestone delivered to Thomas 2nd Earl of Lancaster.

(Wiki-Commons)

In the year 1312, Piers de Gavestone, the son of a Gascon knight and favourite childhood friend of Edward II, turned most of England's nobility into merciless enemies. The Barons were not impressed by the favouritism bestowed on Gavestone, a rude and arrogant man who liked nothing better than to ridicule people, labelling them with derogatory nicknames such as the Earl of Warwick who he nicknamed 'The Black Dog.'

Exasperated, the Barons rebelled and demanded to the King that Gavestone be exiled. Edward refused, so the Barons revolted against the King forcing him to flee to York. Gavestone headed for Scarborough Castle where for some time he defended his position with great bravery. Revengeful, the Barons sieged the castle capturing Gavestone as their prisoner and mounting him on a mule his capturer whispered to him 'you remember me, I am the Black Dog.' In an assembly of Barons, Gavestone was sentenced to death and beheaded in June 1312.

Legend dictates that the ghost of Gavestone haunts Scarborough Castle where people have reported sightings of a headless man wandering around the castle who tries to lure suspecting visitors over the walls to an ignoble death.

*

Sieges at the Castle

Scarborough Castle East

There have been memorable sieges at Scarborough Castle over the years.

One notable one happened during the reign of Queen Mary that personified the phrase 'A Scarborough Warning,' which means 'no warning at all!' This recounts the story behind the words.

In 1554, Mr Thomas Stafford, the second son of Lord Stafford had joined the party of Sir Thomas Wyatt, the Duke of Suffolk. This party feared England becoming re-Catholicised and, combined with the proposed marriage between Mary and Philip of Spain led to the Wyatt Rebellion of 1554. A rebellion led by nobles. Together they forged a plan to surprise the Castle.

Thomas Stafford under disguise strolled into Scarborough on a market day, not attracting any suspicion he could enter the fortress where he walked around casually with a careless air. Soon after thirty of his followers disguised as peasants with market baskets, gained admittance to the Castle; at their earliest opportunity they seized all the sentinels, and after admitting more of their companions (who had concealed weapons), they closed the gate.

Thomas Stafford denounced the Spanish marriage, aware of plans to enslave the English, he called upon the people to rise and styled himself the protector. However, before he sailed from France, his intentions were divulged to the English ambassador. The militia rapidly assembled under the command of Henry Neville, fifth Earl of Westmorland. Stafford with four other insurgents was captured almost without a blow and sent to London, where they were tried and convicted of high treason. Stafford was hanged and quartered at Tyburn on 28 May 1557.

*

The Civil War: The Roundheads and the Royalists

SCARBOROUGH CASTLE.

The Civil wars (1642-1651) were fought between the Roundheads (Parliamentarians) and the Royalists loyal to King Charles 1st (reigned 1625-1649). The Roundheads supported Parliament and believed that Parliament should command supreme control over executive administration. Whereas, in opposition, the Royalists (also called the Cavaliers) claimed to rule by absolute monarchy and the the divine right of Kings.

Throughout this period, Scarborough Castle sustained a long and important siege. At the start of the hostilities, Sir Hugh Cholmley (initially a Parliamentarian but later a Royalist), was governor of the Castle on behalf of the King. Cholmley was born at Roxby Castle, Thornton le Dale, his father was Sir Richard Cholmley and his mother

Susannah (formerly Legard of Ganton Hall). Sir Hugh was knighted in 1626 and elected as a Member of Parliament for Scarborough until the reign of King James 1st who ruled without Parliament for eleven years.

In opposition stood Sir John Meldrum (Parliamentarian), a Scottish soldier of fortune, who had distinguished himself in defence of Hull against the King's forces to succeed Sir William Constable, who had been appointed by Lord Fairfax in command of the siege. Sir John possessed an abundance of endurance and inventiveness and a strong, fervent spirit. He commenced operations on 18th February 1645; storming the town he gained possession of the church. The records of the time support this account of the hostilities;

On February 18th (1645) at around ten o'clock, Scarborough was stormed in four places by English and Scottish soldiers who gained the town and the church. They took eighty-soldiers hostage into the church together with Sir Jordan Crosland who had held Helmsley Castle for the King prior to the civil war.

Sir Hugh Cholmley perceiving the town to be lost had intended to escape by sea in a little pinnace he had there which he called his Running-horse, As a decoy, Sir Hugh secured five Dunkirk vessels lying in the sea road, but to no avail, as Meldrum's cannoneers sank two, and the other three fled. Meldrum got between him and the pinnace and forced him back into the Castle.

Unperturbed, Cholmley and his garrison of men refused to surrender. However, Meldrum had captured from the town and the church thirty-two pieces of artillery, with a store of arms and other prizes, and in the haven one hundred and twenty ships. Nobody on either side expected the castle siege to last twenty-two weeks.

The Parliamentarians prepared for what became a long siege, one of the bloodiest of the civil war, with almost continuous fighting, making the defence tedious and confusing to the attackers, yet the constant battering brought with it much fatigue and sickness. With great determination and loyalty, Sir Hugh's wife Lady Cholmley would not forsake her husband and remained by his side during the whole siege, and because of her presence, she expected Sir Hugh to display empathy and relent, sadly to no avail. Lady Cholmley endured much hardship yet remained resolute and steadfast. Her caring attitude became indefatigable in her attention to the sick.

The fierce battle continued with casualties and fatalities on both sides. However, towards the end of March 1645, Meldrum suffered a setback when he ascended a rock to explore the best position to plant his cannon against the castle. He reached too far, and he was blown over by a massive gust of wind and tumbled down a 200-foot cliff when his cloak acted as a parachute; luckily, he survived the fall, but he was dazed and severely bruised.

Destruction to the great keep failed to end hostilities, on the contrary, a one hundred-ft high wall fifteen-ft thick had fallen onto a sharp narrow approach, which provided the defenders with protection and an arsenal of stone missiles. Meldrum launched attack after attack, but to no avail as during a hand-to-hand battle, he was mortally wounded on 11th May 1645.

The Royalists were hugely outnumbered without any hope of reinforcement or means of escape, thus, Parliament realising the magnitude of this great siege sent strong reinforcement, appointing Sir Matthew Boynton to replace Meldrum, therefore the blockade continued with renewed vigour and enthusiasm.

Although there were longer Civil War sieges elsewhere, none was so intensive, continuous and costlier than that of Scarborough castle. And Scarborough's residents and buildings were to be its victims. The bombardment was so intense that the massive walls of the great tower split in two and half the building collapsed.

After almost a year of gallantly defending the castle, Sir Hugh finally ran out of gunpowder, then money and finally food. The garrison was so weakened by fatigue and a shortage of provisions with many men seized with despair and dying of scurvy. Cholmley had no choice but to surrendered on honourable terms.

The printed terms of the surrender recorded by John Field, London (date unknown.) are as follows; 'Articles agreed and concluded upon the

23rd day of July 1645, between the Hon, Sir Matthew Boynton, Knt, and Bart, one of the Militaries Committee for the Northern Association; Col. Francis Lascelles' Col. Sim. Needham, Commanders in chief for the King and Parliament in Scarborough; and the Hon. Sir Hugh Cholmley, Knt, and Bart. Governor of the Castle there, about the rendition thereof to the persons before named;'

1. That the Castle be surrendered on the 25th day of this instant, July 1645, by twelve of the clock at noon. That all the arms, ordnance, ammunition, provision, and goods, of what sort, soever, now in, and about the Castle (except what is hereafter excepted), shall be delivered to the Commanders in Chief, at Scarborough, or to whom they shall appoint, to the use of the King and Parliament.'

2. That all prisoners now in the Castle be set free within six hours after these articles were sealed.

3. That the governor, Sir Hugh Cholmley, and those officers and gentlemen soldiers, if he desire it, shall have a safe convoy from hence into Holland, or be safely conveyed to Newark, whether they shall choose; and after their coming to Newark, shall then resolve to go into Holland, giving notice thereof within six days, to the Committee for Military Affairs at York, they shall have passes from thence to take the first opportunity of wind and shipping; and such other, who desire passes, shall have them from the said Committee, to go to the King's army, or any of his garrisons, as they please, travelling not above twenty in company, where the Governor or Colonel shall be in person; otherwise not above ten in company; the time to be permitted in their several passes, as the distance of the place to go shall require, none passing through any garrison for the King, if there be another way.

4. That no person going from this Castle be plundered, arrested, or staid upon; and in such case, upon a complaint been made to the Committee at York, to be speedily readdressed.

5. That Lady Cholmley shall have the liberty to live at her own house at Whitby and enjoy such part of her estate as allowed by ordinance of Parliament; that she may have two men-servants, and two horses, to carry herself and such necessary things as granted her.

6. That all inferior officers, common soldiers, and others, with the desire to live at home, shall have passes granted them for that end, and shall not be forced to take up arms against their minds, that the sick and wounded shall be provided for, till their recovery, and then have passes to travel to what place they please, having sufficient time allowed for their journey, and two persons permitted to take care.

7. That the Governor march on his own horse, with a sword, pistols, and defensive arms; and all Field-officers upon their own horses, with their swords and pistols; all Captains and Lieutenants, and Cornets of Horse, in like manner; three servants for the Governor, and one for every Field-officer as, and all other and soldiers on foot, with no other arms than their swords, and not to be compelled to march over ten miles a day.

8. That all officers and soldiers may carry upon their persons what is their own; that nothing be carried in cloak-bags or knapsacks, but their own wearing apparel, writings, evidence, and bills.

9. That every officer, gentleman, or clergyman, may have the liberty to buy or lawfully procure a travelling horse for himself and his servant; that all sick and lame men may enjoy the same privilege.

10. That all gentlemen of quality, and clergymen, have the liberty to march. Gentlemen with their swords; that none carry above the value of 5 shillings in money or plate about their persons and nothing in their cloak-bags, but as expressed in the 8th article.

11. There be no fraud or deceit used, in spoiling or embezzling anything before mentioned or comprised of these articles; and if any of them shall be violated, the party offending shall be delivered to the Commander in Chief where the fact shall be done, to satisfy his offence, and his act shall not be understood as a breach of these articles, nor be prejudicial to any other.

H CHOLMLEY

"We do attest that the within written Articles were signed and sealed by Sir H. Cholmley, in our presence. Tho. Gower, Tho. Crompton Richard Legard."

*

After his surrender, Sir Hugh Cholmley lived in exile, chiefly in France, until June 1649 when his brother Henry pacified Parliament and obtained permission for Sir Hugh to return to England. His wife Elizabeth eventually returned to her house at Whitby where she died in 1655 and then later interned at Peckham-Church in Kent at the feet of her father (Sir William Twisden) in a private choir belonging to the family.

On the 25th of July, the Governor and the survivors witnessed the devastated remains of the church. Only bare wall of the chancel remained, all glass (which had just been restored ten years earlier) had been smashed, the roof full of holes and beyond repair, and the central bell tower weakened and shuddered. The pews (155) had been bedding, shelter or firewood. The overall cost of rebuilding Scarborough's much-loved church was estimated to cost six-hundred pounds, but many items could not be replaced such as St Mary's plait, which Sir Hugh melted down and made into coins to pay his men. He paid them 12 pence a week, by cutting the church's 'silver plate' into coins (crudely) with a basic picture of the castle on one side and the stamped value on the other side with the inscription 'Obsidinm Scarborough 1645'.

These coins ranged from a monetary value of between 6d to half a crown. These rare, valuable coins are often counterfeited. The only pre-war silver plate still belonging to St Mary's is a large cup donated to the church by the Thompson family in 1637.

Further damage to the town during this siege included St Thomas's and four mills. The water conduit was broken up, ships seized or damaged in the port. All these losses were discussed in Parliament by Sir Matthew Boynton and Luke Robinson in November 1646. (Hinderwell, The History of Scarborough.)

*

George Fox. Imprisonment in Scarborough Castle 1665

GEORGE FOX

In 1665, George Fox an English Dissenter and the founder of 'The Religious Society of Friends' or 'Quakers', was imprisoned in the Castle for sixteen-months, due to his religious beliefs. Throughout his imprisonment, he was denied any visitors and slept in a cold, miserable cell overlooking the sea, and a little distance from a spring named 'Lady's Well'. During his atrocious stay at the Castle, Fox wrote his memoir.

Lying much open the wind drove in the rain so forcibly, that the water-saturated his bed and splashed about the room, so much so he often scooped the water from his bed with a platter. For food, he would make a three-penny loaf of bread last three weeks, sometimes longer. Most of the water he drank contained an infusion of wormwood.

The humility and innocuous conduct of George Fox so impressed the governor and officers of the garrison they became friends. Order of the King released George Fox, and this passage was issued during his release.

'Permit the bearer hereof, George Fox, late a prisoner here, but now discharged by his Majesty's order, quietly to pass about his lawful occasions without any molestation given under my hand at Scarborough Castle.'

1st September 1666.

John Crossland, Governor. Scarborough Castle.

*

Lady's Well

Under an arched vault in the Castle yard (near the ruins of the ancient chapel) lies 'Lady's Well' which according to historians (Hinderwell) is consecrated to the Virgin Mary. However, it is difficult to determine the sources of this well and to whom and where its contents were supplied.

In 1746, workmen were ordered to dig a circular trench around the reservoir, in the hope of finding the source. Soon, they discovered several subterraneous drains and channels, for redirecting the rainwater which fell on Castle Hill. This reservoir when filled then contained about 40 tons of water of a very thin consistency and measured one- ounce lighter in the Winchester gallon than any other water in the vicinity.

This water supply was vital to the health and well-being of the soldiers during the sieges of the Castle.

In the mid-1800s Mr William Cockerill, the proprietor of a much-frequented coffee-house, became infamous for a stunt he pulled relating to the water from the 'Lady's Well'. Mr Cockerill was a popular man and well respected within Scarborough Society for his wit and wicked sense of humour and ingenuity.

In his establishment, a salesman had persuaded him to stock 'Bristol Water'. However, unbeknown to the salesman and his customers, Cockerill substituted this water with water from the Lady's Well. This deception was carried out with great ability and involved removing and replacing the wax seal on each bottle before the bottles went on sale. However, during an intoxicating moment, Cockerill inadvertently placed the seal of a Bristol water onto a bottle of sherry. Unfortunately, the seal had no time to cool, and Cockerill's secret was soon discovered.

Cockerill received a severe reprimand for his deception, and for a long time afterwards was obliged to supply water free of charge to all his customers.

*

Monks & Friars

The Cistercians 'The White Friars'. (WikiCommons)

The first Church of St Mary was built in the 12th century, most likely by the masons who built the castle as a place for them to worship. The first documented history of this church is in the year 1189 when Richard Coeur de Lion (Richard the Lionheart) presented it to the Abbey of Citeaux in Normandy. This early church was originally built in the shape of a cross with two towers and a central tower within the Castle walls.

The Cistercians or the 'White Monks' occupied this early church. These monks took their name from Citeaux a village between Dijon and

Chalons in France. The order originated in 1098, fronted by Robert of Molessme, the Abbot of Citeaux. They were called White Monks as they wore a white choir robe over their cassock, unlike the black cuccula which were worn by the Benedictine Monks.

The church was then jointly controlled by the Abbey of Citeaux and the Archbishop of York with mutual consent on the appointment of vicars and met by agreement between both parties.

The Abbey of Citeaux sent three monks to Scarborough to collect taxes and look after the Cistercian interests, while a vicar oversaw the church services and the welfare of the parish. The first vicar Ric. De Chauseye was appointed in 1226.

This important religious order placed great stress on isolation and solitude, and individual poverty. They rejected all feudal revenues and reintroduced manual labour for monks, making it a principal feature of their life.

Grants of land from lay benefactors enabled the order the means to support the community. Rules were agreed to govern the internal affairs of each monastery, Statutes provided by the Citeaux in Burgundy the motherhouse of the Order, regulated the order.

The agreement was that the Abbot should appoint the vicar of St Mary's, and the profits during a vacancy went to the convent. The vicar also swore obedience and headed that he could be removed at the will of the Abbot. No person could erect a chapel in the parish, or an altar in any chapel, under the forfeiture of ten pounds. The claim of the Abbot of the Cistercians, as rector of Scarborough, to the profits of the chapel in the Castle was recognised, and allowed in the fifth year of Edward III, and the custody of the rectory granted to Hugh de Sancho Lupo, 16th of Edward III, on payment of a rent of 35 marks per annum to the Crown.

The church of St Mary remained under the control of the Cistercians for a further two centuries when in the year 1363, the licence granted to the Abbot of the Cistercians for a vicarage house for Henry Bedbebowe, the vicar of Scarborough, and his successor forever.

In the reign of Henry IV, the possessions of the Cistercian Abbey were seized by the King as an 'alien priory'. He granted the custody of the church and advowson of Scarborough, to the prior and convent at Bridlington. (Hinderwell, p.74)

The Cistercians built wonderful gardens, with a walled garden around the church with many wildflowers and unusual plants which resembled paradise. Hence the area is still called 'Paradise'.

*

The Franciscans: The Greyfriars

The Cistercians were one of the four convents to occupy
Scarborough, together with the Franciscan or 'Greyfriars' named
after St. Francis of Assisi, who settled in England in 1224, and in
Scarborough as early as 1239. Peripatetic people, the Cistercians denied
themselves worldly goods. Henry III ordered that the Franciscans should
be entitled to food once a week, and cloth for their robes. Their ankle-
length robes were made from rough grey/brown cloth, hooded, and
worn tied around the waist with a string. The monks could wear no form
of footwear even in winter.

The Franciscans built a Monastery in 1267 when they finally
established themselves in a spacious building on St Sepulchre Street
between Cuckold Hill and Millbeck. (Hinderwell) However, the
Cistercians Friars grew despondent and resented the privileges the
Franciscans were acquiring and bitterly resented their presence in the

town, so much so, they complained to Rome. The Pope instructed the Bishop of Lincoln to demolish the buildings occupied by the Greyfriars. Arguments followed, and both sides were ordered to Rome to discuss their differences before an official.

However, a senior Greyfriar Monk waved all arguments aside declaring, 'If any man will sue thee at the law and take away thy coat, let him have thy cloke also.' He stated on behalf of his brethren that they would give up the place and falling on his knees before the monks prayed pardon for the offence. Mindful that their honour was tarnished, which would place a conspicuous stain on their reputation, the Cistercians halted all operations until they had consulted with the Abbot and the convent of Citeaux.

Following internal consultations, the Greyfriars decided to vacate the site and quit the town, relocating to the parish of Scalby to a rural area called Hatterboard.

In 1958, the Scarborough Archaeological Society excavated open fields on the south side of Lady Edith's Drive (before the building of Scarborough Technological college) to locate the remains of this lost medieval village. They were not disappointed and uncovered the foundations of six houses dating back to 1245.

A grant had been granted for the Greyfriars to construct an aqueduct from springs at Goldus Cliff near Falsgrave, to their convent. This grant also gave the bailiffs of Scarborough the entitlement to two parts of the water supply and the Friars one third. The Friars were expected to share the cost of the maintenance and repair of these pipes, which supplied the local Scarborough community via three troughs, the upper, middle and lower conduits for five-hundred years. In 1847, a part of this ancient watercourse was exposed in St Sepulchre Street between Cukwold Hill and the watercourse named Mill-Beck.

After serving the community of Scarborough with prayers, burials and masses, the Franciscan friary was dissolved in 1539. They are remembered as a well-respected part of Scarborough's history.

*

The Dominican Friars-Carmelites: The Black Friars

DOMINICAN FRIAR

While no vestiges remain of the exact whereabouts of the Dominican convent, we believe it was near Queen Street Methodist Chapel, then called Black Friars Gate, together with a slipway off this known as Friars Entry (now Friars Way). In 1298, the Friars obtained permission to make a new street to their church within the town wall named Cross Street.

The land at Friars Entry became a burial ground. In 1826, several mutilated burial urns were uncovered by a man named Jerimiah Barton who while digging in the cellar in Friars Entry he discovered a significant number of human bones?

The Dominicans had rigid rules and were expected to live in perpetual silence. It was frowned upon to converse in conversation without the permission of the superior. Reading sacred scriptures, the monks devoted themselves to prayer. They were restricted to almost continual fasting, especially between the 11th September to Easter. 'Black Friars' was so named due to their clothing, a black cloak over their vestments and down to their heels, unlike other orders, they wore boots and refrained from walking around the town barefoot.

*

The connection with St Mary's Church and the monastery continued until the reign of Edward III when the patronage passed into the King's hands. In 1408, Richard II donated it to the prior and convent of Bridlington, in whose hands it remained until the suppression of the monasteries by Henry VIII, when between March and May 1539 all the orders were disbanded, convents seized, thus ending the habitation of the Friars in Scarborough.

Between them, the Friars left behind a positive, long-lasting legacy for medieval Scarborough. Sadly, no longer would the barefooted black, white, or grey friars be walking through the narrow streets of Scarborough. Their convents were abandoned only to crumble and decay.

*

The Churches of Scarborough:

St Mary's Parish Church

Dating back to the year 1000, and before the Norman Conquest, it is probable that a small Saxon chapel existed within the partly ruined walls of the Roman signal station, and long before the building of a castle. Possibly, a beacon chapel, whose priests might act as coast-watchers and light-keepers to protect the Saxon shore. Around this time, a small fishing community settled around the harbour below the headland. In 1066 the settlement and the small chapel were ransacked and burnt by Earl Tostig.

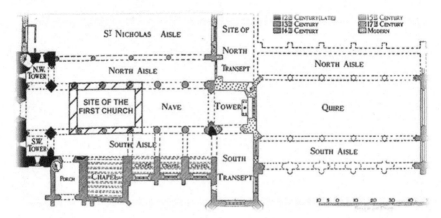

Illustration reproduced from the Victoria History of the Country of York, North Riding 1914.

The ancient Church of St Mary stands majestically on the high ground leading to the Castle. Perhaps once a conventual or monastic church, with its churchyard crowded with tombs.

Scarborough's community grew quickly; to accommodate the increasing congregation, extensions were added to the church. First additions were imposing twin towers, followed by north and south aisles. The foundation walls of the first church-supported three of the nave's five circular solid pillars on the north side and three of the five solid pillars on the south side.

During the 'great siege' the church suffered severe damage, the transept shook rendering it unstable, and the tower fell onto the nave in 1659, reducing the church to a state of ruin. Ten years later, following contributions from the parish, the church was partially repaired on the fabric of the old building.

1848-Restoration

The church was again restored in October 1848, when within the south-west tower several interesting artefacts including a shrine made from fine white gypsum or alabaster was discovered. On several pillars in the nave traces of original paintings were unearthed, which unfortunately, were aged and damaged through time making it impossible to ascertain the subjects of the scripture's history.

Opposite the choir near to the east end of the south aisle, revealed the remnants of a large iron crook or a gate-band, together with an archway leading into the south transept. To the west of the transept two low arches probably the resting places of the founders of the chantry were uncovered.

Beneath these lay two stone coffins with a few decomposed bones in each and most probably from the Middle-Ages. On the wall above these coffins marked a cross and other scribbles denoting the words; 'Ora Pro Nobis.'

Also discovered were Old Testament tables with crosses and moulded stones.

The church was reopened on Thursday 25th July 1850. The sermon was preached by the Archbishop of York and the newly restored church was packed full of worshipers who much admired the renovations.

*

St Nicholas Church

This ancient church no longer exists but was built in the year 1175, on St Nicholas Cliff, between the entrance to Cliff-Bridge and the museum. There are no remains of this ancient church, but bones have been found on the site, (Hinderwell) and a small brass plate inscribed 'Fr. Wills de Thornton' with part of an inscription on the reverse is now in the Rotunda Museum. (British History Online)

St Thomas's Church

EAST FRONT OF ST. THOMAS'S CHURCH.

Credit S.W. Theakston

St Thomas Church was a spacious building at Newburgh Gate. In 1788 the site became the home to the workhouse. There were houses adjacent to the workhouse which charged a small annual church rent for encroachments on the churchyard. At the time of Leyland's itinerary (1538) this edifice is noted as a 'great Chappelle'. At the side of Newborough Gate, was once a chapel of ease to the parish, as church records show that four churchwardens were annually elected, and the repairs to the church in 1642 were affected by an assessment of the whole parish. This church was converted into a magazine by Sir John Meldrum, during the great siege of 1644, and demolished by fire from the garrison. In 1649 it was ordered by the bailiffs and burgesses that: 'Upon consideration, that part of St Thomas church has already fallen-down, and the rest is ready to fall, and evil-dispossessed people have stolen much of the timber and slates to the roof. Therefore, for prevention of further embezzlement, the church should be taken down, and the materials sold to the best advantage and the monies arising should go to the cost of repairs to St Mary's church.'

*

St Nicholas Church (St Nicholas Cliff)

No vestiges remain of St Nicholas Church, which existed in the reign of Henry II. This ancient church was on the land on St Nicholas Cliff to the north of Cliff Bridge, which has since eroded. The terrace, cleared and levelled in 1791, uncovered a complete skeleton undisturbed in the cliff, the same vicinity to where this church stood. The teeth and skull of this skeleton were preserved. Also found in 1810 was a copper tombstone bearing the name Frater William de Thornton, who lived fifty years after the Church of St Nicholas.

Christ Church

Credit S.W Theakston

Christ Church was in Vernon Place (Now Vernon Road) and erected by public subscriptions, and by a generous sum from the Parliamentary Commissioners of three-thousand pounds. The church was completed in October 1826 and consecrated on 23rd August 1828 by the Archbishop of York. The stone for building the church was given by Sir JVB Johnstone, Bart; of Hackness. The church seated between 1200 and 1300 people, one half in pews and the reminder free benches, including an upper galley at the west end for the children of the Amicable Society, and other schools connected with the establishment.

Anne Bronte and the Robinson family worshipped here, and Anne's funeral was conducted here before horse-drawn carriage transported her coffin to her final resting place in St Mary's churchyard.

The area where Christ Church was situated is now home to Wacker's fish & chip shop and Iceland frozen foods.

*

Dissenters & Meeting Houses

Independent Meeting House (Presbyterian)

During the Victorian era, there were numerous dissenters' meeting houses in Scarborough. The oldest of them was the Independent Meeting House (Presbyterian) which was in St Sepulchre's Street, built in the year 1703; and rebuilt in 1774. Theakston reports in his book Theakston's guide to the Scarborough (1856) that 'this church stood on the ground connected with the possessions, if not the residence of the Knights Hospitallers' (who had made a grant to the Franciscan convent). This chapel accommodated 600-700 followers. The pastorate for fifty-eight years was Rev. S. Bottomley who died in 1831 aged 80. Several monuments are placed on the walls of this church in memory of Rev Bottomley. The first minister was Rev WM Hanney who, with his father, was persecuted by Charles II during his victimisation of Presbyterians.

Friends (Quakers)

Photo Credit Gravestone Photographic Research.

The first meeting of Friends (Quakers) in Scarborough was in the year 1651 at Low Conduit Street when it is said that George Fox and his associates discovered the religion they had been seeking. They soon needed larger premises and moved to Carr Street (now Eastborough). This meeting place had a balcony which is where George Fox gave a speech in 1651.

In 1801, the friends needed more space and moved to a building opposite the Independent Meeting-House courtesy of the 'shipbuilding family the Tindall's who were also Friends'. In line with their beliefs, this building was plain and simple in appearance. This building still exists but is now two separate private houses. However, the stones shown in this picture in the front garden which were quite possibly gravestones must have been moved at some time. Many prominent Scarborough merchants who were 'Friends' were treated with suspicion, and contempt and often ridiculed merely for their beliefs.

Ebenezer Chapel is the oldest of the three Methodist churches and established in Scarborough in 1771. Its first minister William Hague was born in Malton and came to Scarborough at the age of twenty where he worked as a sailor for three years. Educating himself to read and write he took rooms on the sands where he preached the Gospel and converted many to the ways of God; so much so that he applied to Bridlington for permission to build a chapel in Scarborough.

Permission granted; the first Ebenezer Chapel opened in April 1777. This chapel soon became too small for the increasing number of followers and was enlarged three times. Hague stayed as minister for 48 years and died at the age of 94.

The foundation stones of the chapel on Longwestgate were laid and the building opened on August 12th, 1827, seating 900 people. Known as 'Baptist Chapel' the property sold at auction in November 1949 for two-thousand-five-hundred pounds. The buyer Mr Boothby a battery manufacturer, intended to carry on his business in the building. The adjoining institute and caretaker's house sold to The York & District Deaf & Dumb Benevolent Society for thirteen hundred pounds. The purchasers intended to provide a centre for deaf and dumb people in Scarborough.

Ebenezer Chapel closed in 1947, and services transferred to the Columbus Ravine Church.

*

The Primitive Methodists

Hugh Bourne and William Clowes, both from Hull, set up a Primitive Methodist meeting house at no 4 Globe Street in 1821. A church established on the site, and once used by the Franciscans, was called the Holy Church of St Sepulchre. This church could seat up to 1200 people. In 1861, the Jubilee Methodists church opened in Aberdeen Walk, and the building filled with followers most Sundays, but numbers decreased during the war years.

Wesleyan Methodist Chapel

Photograph credit Queen Street Church Scarborough

In the year 1757, the Wesleyan's came to Scarborough. A preacher called Thomas Brown secured a room on Whitehead Hill, and then moved to a place known as 'Bennets Entry' which was in the passage leading from Cross Street to Dumple Street. The market hall is now a part of this site.

In 1772, they bought land in Church Stairs Street and erected a chapel to seat 600 people. John Wesley spoke these words from these stairs;

'If you want the model of a chapel for beauty and neatness, go to Scarborough, it is plain, yet one of the most elegant preaching-houses in England.' (Wesley)

However, this church did not last too long, as in 1813, a new chapel was founded at Bird Yard on Cross Street, and the Church Stairs Chapel was pulled down.

As numbers continued to grow, it was soon necessary to find larger premises. In 1840 a large chapel was built in Queen Street named Centenary Chapel previously the site of The Blacksmiths Inn. The cost of the building was seven-thousand pounds, three thousand of which came from subscriptions and church collections. The church had 500 seats free to the poor of the town. Underneath the church were school rooms and an apartment for the minister. This church was well attended and became the 'mother church' for many of the other chapels. The building suffered damage in the First World War and was destroyed in the 1915 fire to Boyes 'The Rem' warehouse, which was next door. The church was reduced to ashes. However, in 1923 the church was rebuilt, and to this day the Queen Street Church continues to thrive.

The Wesleyans also had a small chapel in George Street (near the jail) which opened in 1847. Demand for a seat was so high that in the late 1860s the Wesleyans bought a plot of land opposite the Railway station known then as Newton's Field (re-named Belle-Vue Square). The foundation stone was laid by Henry Fowler, a Wesleyan solicitor and ship-owner.

Throughout the mid-nineteenth century, religion flourished in Scarborough and other churches were established there including The Plymouth Brethren on Merchants Row, and The Bethel Mission Chapel on Sandside, which was the old Town Hall. This church was popular with fishermen and their families.

Batty Alley Chapel

This chapel was formerly the chapel of the Free Church Wesleyan, which was opened in 1867 by the town missionary.

Bethel Mission

Formerly the old Town Hall and attended mainly by fishermen and their families. The services conducted by Wesleyan, Independent, and Primitive Methodist denominations. Services were held twice a week on Tuesday and Saturday evenings.

St Thomas Chapel of Ease

A chapel of ease was erected on East Sandgate in 1839 in the name of St Thomas. The first stone was laid on 21st December 1939 by widow Mrs Ann Woodall in the presence of the mayor and the building completed the following year through subscriptions and a grant of three hundred pounds from the Independent Society for Building Churches. The overall building cost was two-thousand pounds. This church was constructed predominantly for the poor, who often found the proximity of the parish church inconvenient or crowded. This Episcopal Chapel was opened on 17th October 1840 by the Archbishop of York. Entry was a ticket to the subscribers who had made the building possible. This chapel closed between 1965 and 1968 and is now a Grade 2 listed building.

Catholics

The Catholics first worshipped in the Apple Market (King Street) then at a church on Westgate which according to Hinderwell had no large congregation. The first priest in Scarborough was the Rev. James Seyne, who was there from 1826 to 1831.

Suitable premises were acquired in Auborough Street, and in 1835 Canon Walker was appointed to Scarborough, and for 40 years he devoted himself to the work of the mission. He opened a school for the children of the congregation in his own house and enlarged the chapel. Finding the accommodation still insufficient, he erected a new church and converted the old chapel into schools.

The church of St Peter was begun in 1856 on Castle Road and is now a grade 2 listed building.

*

Over the years, there have been numerous churches in Scarborough. Unfortunately, I cannot mention them all but, all visitors to Scarborough were most welcome to attend church services at any denomination they chose. The only church that charged visitors for their church services was Christ Church.

*

The Spaw

Scarborough: The Queen of the Watering Places

Poetical Sketches of Scarborough 1813

Scarborough owes its popularity as a much-admired seaside resort to one of its residents Mrs Thomasine Farrer who in the year 1620 discovered mineral waters on the beach. Mrs Farrer was a well-respected gentlewoman, whose family resided at Wykeham Abbey. Her father Edward Hutchinson was at one time a member of parliament for Scarborough. Mrs Farrer's sister Isabelle was married to one of the Thompsons who was an integral part of Scarborough history. Thomasine's husband John was senior Bailiff at Scarborough in 1613 and had set up a hospital in Low Conduit Street to accommodate as many poor widows as the premises could reasonably provide.

Mrs Farrer liked nothing better than to stroll on the south bay of Scarborough sands. One day she stopped just under the cliffs at Driple Cotes when she noticed spring waters bubbling over russet-brown coloured stones. Inquisitively, Mrs Farrer tasted the water and found it tasted acidic and different from that of other springs. Her curiosity fuelled she took some of the water to her home and bravely tested it herself, she then persuaded friends and family to do the same. They found the waters to contain medicinal qualities. Once she communicated her findings publicly people soon came from far and wide to Scarborough to test the newly discovered 'curative' waters.

Scarborough was soon on the map as a 'health spa' town; the waters were so famous that the town burgesses passed a by-law prohibiting the precious waters from being transported away in barrels by land or sea. By 1727 the cost of the spa waters had risen to one shilling per 40 litres and sixpence when bottled and sold locally. The town bailiffs profited from the sale of the waters.

Mrs Farrer may have been responsible for finding the waters, but it was Robert Wittie, the son of a former mayor of Beverley who brought the medicinal qualities of the waters to the area.

Dr Wittie studied medicine at Kings College Cambridge before returning to Hull. Believing in the medicinal qualities of the Scarborough water, in 1667 he wrote a book entitled 'Scarborough- Spaw' which he addressed to 'The Right Hon, and truly noble lords, James, Earl of Suffolk, and John, Lord Roos, son and heir-apparent to the Earl of Rutland.' (Hinderwell)

According to Wittie the waters 'hath their virtues from its participation in vitriol, iron, sulphur, alum, nitrate and salt.' (Wittie, 1667)

The Spa consisted of two springs namely, the north & south wells. The north, a mineral spring used as a mineral tonic or chalybeate water for the relief of nervous diseases and hysteria, while the more important south well was 'more of a tonic and aperient.' (Shaw) The south well claimed to cure a variety of diseases, especially of the bowels and kidneys.

Wittie claimed that taking a small glass of the south well water a couple of times a day, was more effective than many powerful medicines, especially when prepared with a small piece of Scarborough salt, or a glass of seawater.

Furthermore, Dr Richard Mead (founder of Great Ormond Street Hospital) an eminent London physician of the day wrote, 'These waters, fraught with virtues formerly known to few, and healing chiefly the sick inferior rank, are at length, by your experience and subsequent just and generous recommendations of them introduced into better company, and now cheer the spirits and brace the nerves of Peers as well as Commoners.' (Hinderwell)

This statement opened the floodgates that invited Dukes, Marquises, Earls, and Barons to the now popular 'watering place' of Scarborough.

Reports suggest that during the Civil War (1642-51) visitors to the town were limited and that during the siege(s) at the Castle sick, wounded soldiers found relief from the waters to help relieve the symptoms of scurvy and other diseases.

Dicky Dickinson & The Old Wooden Spaw

THE OLD WOODEN SPA

(Rowntree)
The Spaw Wells
Soon as the sun's resplendent ray
Breaks oe'r the foreland into day
Light as the vapours that exhale
From mountains height, or skim the vale,
The nymphs arise-each lovely face
Beams with a renovated grace;
And charms are witness'd, that adorn
None but the daughters of the morn.

'Tis now the busy crowd prepares
A visit to the Spa-Well stairs:
For health, like truth, as sagas tell,
Lies at the bottom of a well;
And he who built this fabric knew
The object we should hold in view;
So very wisely thought it fit,
We take some steps to dip for it.
(1813)

The first cistern for this coveted medicinal water was erected in 1698, it was nothing fancy, just a basic wooden structure designed purely for the dispensing of the waters to ladies and gentlemen of quality who were able to spend three months a year at Scarborough 'curing' themselves from the indulgence of the other nine.

An attempt was made to expand on the popularity of the waters and erect a 'Spa'. The Corporation appointed Mr Dicky Dickinson as the governor of this spa, and a lease allowed him to rent for a small fee two tenements and a staithe called Dripple Cote for seven years.

Dicky Dickinson was a likeable man with substantial wit and a vibrant personality. Deformed by a congenital disability he spoke with a speech impediment, but nothing stood in his way of performing his duties the best way he could. His business acumen was outstanding, and despite his 'different' appearance, he had many female admirers. Dicky was not interested in affairs of the heart and compared his aficionados to that of the spa clock saying my clock is 'too forward just like you!'

Upon entering Dicky's house to taste the waters you had to pay five shillings for men and two shillings for the season and sign Dicky's book. After this, you could come and go as you pleased, and many people flocked to taste the waters, as they did to Bath and Tunbridge Wells.

Unfortunately, this did not last long as in 1735 the staithe of the spaw was washed down by a strong tide, and in December 1737 disaster struck in what was believed to be an earthquake. However, it was most probably a landslip resulting from erosion of the coastline; almost an acre of land slipped down the cliff taking with it five cows grazing (they survived). Simultaneously, a fire broke out in the ladies' quarters burning this part of the building to the ground. This misfortune not only buried Dicky's house but also buried the precious spring.

Fortunately, the springs were located and cleaned, and the spaw started again. Although losing his house and the stress of losing his business was all too much for Dicky, he could not get over 'the earthquake' and he died in 1738.

Spaw Waters

SCARBOROUGH - SPAW.

Whereas by an Accident which happened to the Spaw at Scarborough about Christmas last, the Publick have been deprived of the Benefit of the Spaw Water for these three Months past; We, the Bailiffs of Scarborough, do hereby give Notice, That the Springs being, after a great deal of Labour and Expence, intirely recovered, all Gentlemen, and Dealers, may be supplied with any Quantity of

Scarborough - Spaw Water

They shall have Occasion for, by writing as usual to their Correspondents at this Place: And We do hereby assure the Publick, that the building of the Spaw-Houses being already begun, there will be all proper Accommodations finish'd against the ensuing Season : As witness our Hands,

Scarborough, Apr.   James Hebden,⎫ Bailiffs of
18, 1738.   Francis Goland,⎭ Scarborough.

And next Week will be publish'd,
Price Half a Crown
(Dedicated to the Royal Society)
THREE COPPER PLATES,
exactly grav'd and taken on the Spot; being a Survey of the Spaw at Scarborough, before the Fall of the Cliffs ; a View of the same immediately after the Accident, and a Survey of the Spaw as it now stands since the Recovery of the Springs.
Sold by Ward and Chandler Booksellers at Scarborough, and in Coney-street, York; and at the Ship without Temple-Bar, London.

Stamford Mercury 27th April 1738.

Following the landslide, neighbouring towns like Bridlington tried to profit from the town's disaster. Declaring that the Scarborough water had a blackish taste to it.

Scarborough held its own and although quite a considerable distance from its main rival, Bath, Scarborough innkeepers stood their ground fought back and kept coaches which ran between the spa towns. Other visitors came by sea, which was a cheaper but a less favourable form of travel, taking four or five days from London.

Eventually, the roads were rebuilt especially the turnpike in the Great North Road which improved the road between York and Scarborough.

In 1739, at the expense of the corporation, the spaw was rebuilt. Five years later, the season started in July and was therefore short. By this time the drinking room of the spa and the paths around it were rough and dirty. One visitor described it as 'A dirty ill built and very badly paved town.' The dispensing of the waters continued until after the First World War, but, by that time, they were quite an incidental attraction; times were changing, the clientele expected more, thus more emphasis was put on music, dancing and sea-bathing.

*

Sea Bathing & The Seaside

Scarborough saw the first bathing machine in 1735. A horse-drawn carriage on wheels would take the bather out to sea where they could discreetly undress and enter the water.

Doctors advised that a healthy male should take a dip in the sea five minutes before breakfast each day.

Credit Digital Library of America.

However, a female (the weaker sex), invalids and children housekeeper to take no more than three dips in the sea for two minutes three hours after breakfast, no more than three times a week.

Two attendants and a boy to take the carriage to the water would help the females to get themselves prepared for their dip in the sea, while men had one boy to guide the horse and one attendant.

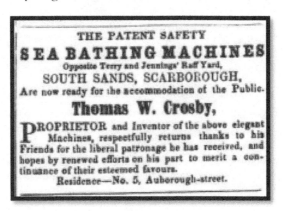

Scarborough Mercury 1858

This all changed in 1871 when it was deemed unnecessary for so many people (and animals) to be employed for simply someone taking a 'dip' in the sea. By 1904, the Corporation installed bathing tents on the North Bay beyond the Spa.

Britain's First Seaside Resort

In 25th May 1871, 'The Bank Holiday Act' pioneered by the MP for Maidstone Mr John Lubbock came into force, whereby all Banks in the United Kingdom on Easter Monday, Whitsuntide Monday, the first weekday in August, would close. For the first-time workers around the country had time on their hands to relax and pursue leisure time and escape to the seaside.

The railway had made travel more accessible for workers from the Yorkshire mill towns to escape the mundane, the smoke and the fog, and head to Scarborough which had everything for the wholesome family holiday.

Scarborough Town Hall advertised the resort as 'the perfect tonic holiday' ideal for the mind and body, with clean air, sunshine and miles of golden sands with endless entertainments, including cricket matches, cricket festival, and open-air theatres. There were grand hotels, affordable boarding houses, piers, theatres, shows, sand, sea, ice-cream and fish and chips, and later in the 1950s even a mechanical elephant which held eight people travelled at a speed of 5 mph and waggled both its tail and trunk.

*

The Poor & The Workhouse

Before introducing the new poor law, impoverished people were provided for under the Elizabethan poor law of 1601 whereby, wealthier residents of the community paid rates to support the less fortunate. This arrangement allowed the poor to receive an 'outdoor allowance' enabling them to still live in their own home and not rely on food and shelter from the workhouse. As wide-spread poverty worsened, resentment festered within the upper-classes who despised having to pay towards the keep of the less fortunate. Some wealthy people took the stance that many of the poor were lazy and that by giving away handouts to poor people they would have no incentive to better themselves. The hierarchy thought that the present system was far too lenient and did not encourage the poor to seek work.

Scarborough's Poor

Scarborough tried to look after the poor of the town as best it could. Numerous benefactors provided money for the impoverished, together with various charitable collections especially in winter, which was for many long, cold and miserable.

The Amicable Society

The Amicable Society was founded in the year 1729 by Robert North, Esq the son of a vicar and quite an extrovert, yet a man of exemplary benevolence and piety. North had spent many years working abroad, his conversation was emphatic, and he possessed great wit.

The society had over 200 members who provided clothing and schooling for the children of the poor. The intention of the Amicable

Society was for 'preserving the children from the contagion of vicious examples and lead them into the path of holiness and social duty, to ensure that they will not be victims of profligacy and pests to society.' (Cole, 1825)

Scarborough Corporation gave land to the Amicable Society for the building of a schoolhouse; this land near Duesbery's Walk to the north of Queen Street, was where 78 children were clothed and educated.

Trinity House

Trinity House, built-in 1602 contained 27 apartments which by all accounts were poorly constructed and not well ventilated. As a result, in 1832 the building had to be rebuilt at a cost of sixteen-hundred pounds funded by voluntary subscriptions. This building was situated on St Sepulchre Street and opposite to where the Primitive Methodist Chapel was. The house was exclusively for 'worn out and disabled mariners and their families'.

The Seamen's Hospital

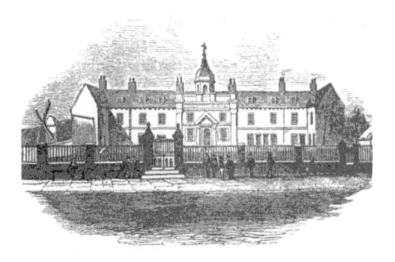

SEAMEN'S HOSPITAL.

Credit S.W Theakston

The Seamen's Hospital was erected in 1752, by the shipowners of Scarborough for the use of aged and disabled seamen, their wives and children. Funding for this hospital was supported by the owner of every ship belonging to the Port of Scarborough, who contributed sixpence for each person on board at the time the ship was out at sea and in actual service.

This hospital was a 'great commodious building' situated in Castle Road to the north of the town. The hospital had a central building with two wings which had 36 apartments, and a spacious green in front. In addition to accommodation, the hospital provided aid to 150 non-residents from the fund.

In 1884, The Seaman's Hospital was the subject of a serious enquiry and at the centre of a 'Meat Poisoning investigation'. 74-year- old William Newby, a retired mariner who lived at the hospital with his wife, had purchased some brawn from Mr John Whitaker, an eating- housekeeper whose shop was on Newborough. Shortly after eating the brawn Mr Newby fell violently sick as did his wife. His wife was seriously ill but recovered, but Mr Newby was not so lucky and died two days later. An inquest was held at the Town Hall as 28 other cases were also reported. Mr Whitaker gave evidence stating that normally he made his own brawn as there was no shortage of pigs' heads, feet, and offal at Scarborough market, but on this occasion, he had purchased the brawn in tins from a Mr Smith of Bradford. The coroner gave evidence and indicated that the brawn had been analysed and found to be 'unwholesome', and the meat was not fresh when cooked. The verdict recorded death by rotten meat, and Mr Whitaker wholly exonerated from any blame in the matter.

A few years later in 1899, The Seaman's Hospital again came under scrutiny. Mrs Sarah Stork, the wife of William Stork a master mariner died in room 24 at the Seaman's Hospital.

The inquest invited the jury to see the room where the deceased lady resided. Poor Mrs Stork's body had been found naked on the floor. The room was in a filthy deplorable state due to the lady's state of health. It seems that she had no assistance and no supervision. The jury concluded that nobody should be expected to live in such a terrible state. The coroner stated that he had visited the lady's room and was appalled by what he saw and said that the stench to the room was 'poisonous', so much so he could not get the aroma out of his nose.

Taylor's Free Dwellings

Established in 1817 due to the generosity of Mr Joseph Taylor who left the sum of one thousand pounds in his will for building a house for the elderly and respectable poor rent-free. Joseph Taylor was a Quaker who also bequeathed the sum of one hundred pounds for the education of boys in the town, together with a 'coal charity' which provided free coal for eighty needy families throughout winter.

Wilson's Mariners Asylum

Richard Wilson Esq was born in Scarborough in 1764. The son of a shipowner, he spent many years at sea before becoming Chief Magistrate for Scarborough in the years 1817, 1822, and 1831. He married Mary Dowker a lady of great empathy and who had great beauty. Unfortunately, Mary died unexpectedly, leaving Richard heartbroken.

Richard wanted to bequeath something for the benefit of his hometown. In his will, he left a sum of money to build houses suitable for 'decayed or disabled mariners, shipowners, their wives and widows.' A plot of land was found near North Cliff and fourteen dwelling- houses were erected in the then-modern style of 'Domestic gothic of the Elizabethan age.'

In 1879 Captain Thomas Luccock and his wife Sarah were selected to reside in one of Wilson's alms-houses and soon moved into number 11. However, they soon turned out to be unsuitable as residents due to Sarah's eccentric behaviour, which upset her neighbours. Sarah was addicted to alcohol and once inebriated had a violent and aggressive nature and an abusive vocabulary. In the spring of 1880, the warden complained of Sarah's offensive manner to her neighbour Mary Bone regarding their shared passage yard and water tap closet. Soon after many other of the alms-house's occupants complained about the conduct of the Luccocks, especially when on Boxing Day the same year Sarah hammered on her neighbour's door cursing at them at length then spreading herself across their doorstep refusing to move. When she did eventually return to her own house, she attacked her sleeping husband with a broomstick and a bucketful of cold water. Once sober, Sarah's defence was that her husband drove her to drink by refusing to give her a kiss and a cuddle. The trustees were not impressed and gave the couple notice to quit.

*

The Workhouse

The new poor law first introduced in 1834, demanded that parishes were grouped into unions, and each union was to provide a workhouse to accommodate their paupers. The Scarborough workhouse encompassed the north riding and covered the areas between East Ayton and Wykeham.

The government wanted the workhouses to be unpleasant to encourage people not to want to go back and to better themselves. Each workhouse had a board of guardians who were elected (prominent) male residents. This board of guardians oversaw the running of the workhouse and decided on applications etc. The day to day running was overseen by a master and a matron who both were required to live on the premises. Often, the decision to enter the workhouse would be not only last resort, but also your only option, especially for the elderly who had no savings to fall back on, and who could no longer work.

The regime of the workhouse was strict, you would never want to return and would work hard to avoid it. All 'inmates' had to wear a uniform. Male and females were segregated, and families split up. There was a rigid timetable, and all inmates were expected to work hard and carry out physically demanding work.

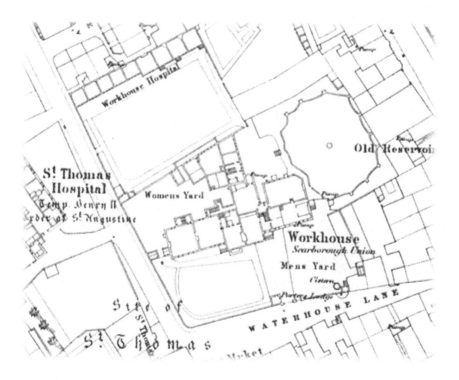

The Original Workhouse 1850

The original workhouse in Scarborough was on the north side of Newborough Street on Waterhouse Lane. It was an old dilapidated building. Initially, the new Poor Union intended to use this existing building and spent over three-hundred pounds in refurbishment to enable it to accommodate 170 people. In 1842, an adjacent prison block was converted to provide for vagrants, and a fever ward administered by St Thomas Hospital under the burgesses of Scarborough was added in 1847. The workhouse yard and gardens which formed part of the hospital were formerly the burial ground of St Thomas church.

One of the original residents of this old workhouse was Miss Margaret Screeton who died in the workhouse in December 1833; she was 103 years old. This grand old lady had no choice but to enter the workhouse as she had a dislocated hip, no medical care, and no financial means, but she had retained all her faculties and before this injury had walked for 7-10 miles each day. She often told the tale of how she remembered being in Carlisle with her mother in the year 1745 during the Scottish Rebellion when she remarked that she was 'A grand strong wench.'

Another inmate, Miss Jane Hall first entered Scarborough Workhouse in 1797 when she was just twenty-three years old. She died in July 1847 aged seventy-three. Jane had never married but had four children all born in the Workhouse, three of the children died and were no doubt taken to the 'Dead House' in Dean Road (a small Victorian mortuary where the dead from the Workhouse and Prison went before burial). Jane's fourth child, a daughter, lived in and out of the workhouse most of her life. Like her mother, she never married, but again had four children, but three died. Her surviving child, a son, broke the cycle and went to sea and did not follow his family tradition of living his life in poverty. Following Jane's death, calculations confirmed that this 'family of paupers' had cost the union up to one- thousand pounds, which at that time was frowned upon severally by the community.

*

Scarborough's New Workhouse

In 1858 an advertisement was placed in local newspapers inviting tenders for building a new workhouse in Scarborough. Between 20-30 plans were received by The Board of Guardians. The plans were removed to a large room at Trinity House as there was more room to view the submitted proposals. The contract went to Architects George & Henry Styan of York. An advert to acquire builders appeared in the Scarborough Mercury in September 1858, and work on the new building commenced soon after.

TO BUILDERS

NEW WORKHOUSE

The Board of Guardians of the Scarborough Union are desirous of receiving TENDERS FOR THE ERECTION OF A WORKHOUSE in Scarborough, from the 7th to the 20th of October next, both inclusive between the hours of 10 a.m. and 4 p.m.; and Bills of Quantities may be obtained, and any information, on application to Mr Styan, Architect, York.

Sealed Tenders endorsed "Tenders for Workhouse" must be sent on or before the 20th of October 1858, addressed to me. Security will be required for the due performance of the work, and the Board do not bind themselves to accept the lowest or any Tender.

By Order of the Board

EDWARD. S. DONNER

Clerk to the Union.

Scarborough. September 18th, 1858.

Illustrated London News 1860

The new workhouse opened on 4th December 1859 when its first residents were the aged paupers transported from the old dilapidated workhouse to their 'new home'. The first master was twenty-seven-year-old Richard Harrison, who with his wife, a cook, matron, infirmary nurse and a porter ran this new establishment with 92 initial inmates (there was room for 200-300 inmates). The entrance consisted of large white bricks over which was a large shield with the Scarborough Arms engraved on it. It must have been a lasting memory to those with the misfortune to enter through it.

By 1896, it was considered by some of the Board of Guardians that the Workhouse had exhausted its useful life. It was overcrowded, and the infirmary was not fit for purpose.

Sir Charles Legard, the chairman of the board, argued that an extension to the infirmary together with other minor improvements were vital. Other members suggested that it would be more economical to build a new workhouse on a more extensive site to accommodate 300-350 inmates, perhaps on the outskirts of the town and to include a self-sufficient farm. The argument was that the country's poor were not improving their positions and that the board should look towards not just the next 50 years, but the next 100 years.

*

By 1930, came the abolition of the Board of Guardians system. Scarborough Workhouse became Scarborough Public Assistance Institution. In 1936, 20 beds were added to accommodate mental health patients. The vagrant's ward closed in 1940. In 1948, the site became St Mary's Hospital, which closed in 2000.

*

Tragic Tales from the Scarborough Workhouse

The Government at the time feared encouraging 'idleness'. Therefore, they intentionally made the conditions in the workhouse as grim as they could. The Guardians made sure that all would fear the workhouse and it would only be used as a last resort, so people would feel ashamed and embarrassed to walk through the formidable workhouse gates.

The Guardians believed that 'Pauperism' was in the blood. Therefore, to discourage the children of the poor from following in their impoverished parents' footsteps, they were encouraged to be useful God-fearing members of the community. Sometimes, it just didn't happen that way. During times of high unemployment, entry into the workhouse was high as work became scarce. Unmarried pregnant girls and the elderly or sick were often disowned by their own families and had no money for hospitals or medication, so they had no alternative, but to enter the workhouse.

*

Throughout the years of the Scarborough Workhouse, there have been many heartbreaking stories of life inside the establishment; these are just a few.

In July 1885 two staff members of Scarborough Workhouse appeared before the Scarborough Court, charged with causing the death of five-year-old David Dunhill, the son of labourer Elliot Dunhill. David died at Scarborough Workhouse due to scalding while being bathed. Evidence showed that boys under seven had a bath every Saturday night. This Saturday Richard Atkinson and William Garnett prepared the bath for young David, both men were experienced in this duty.

The bathtub was filled with six buckets of hot water and two buckets of cold. Neither employee tested the temperature of the water. First in the water was five-year-old David. He screamed and immediately jumped out. Annoyed, Atkinson put the terrified child straight back in the scalding water. David screamed again shouting that the water was too hot. Atkinson took no notice and thrust the boy back down taking hold of his hands and legs. The water was so hot that the skin fell off the poor boy's arms, legs and thighs. A second boy was placed in the same water soon after. This boy, while still alive, had not sufficiently recovered from his injuries to give evidence in court.

Tragically, poor David never recovered and died the following day.

The Master of the workhouse Mr White said he was in no doubt that the water was too hot. The jury found by thirteen to one that Atkinson was guilty of the manslaughter of David Dunhill, and he was taken into custody. The jury severally reprimanded Mr Garnett but released him without charge.

The Workhouse Master

In 1907, the Workhouse Master was fifty-five-year-old Robert Metcalfe, who originated from Pickering. Previously, he had worked as a draper's assistant for his wife's father in the family business. He became assistant Workhouse Master for Scarborough in 1890 and later Master in 1892. In the early hours of Tuesday 10th April 1907 despite a thorough search, Mr Metcalfe could not be found. He was last seen by his wife and daughter at tea-time when he took tea with them. The following morning, one of the aged paupers also a gardener went into one greenhouse and was shocked to find Mr Metcalfe hanging by a rope. He was dead. At the time no reason could be given for this rash act.

Mr Metcalfe was a well-known figure around Scarborough, some of his friends reported that in recent weeks before his death he was 'much troubled'. There was great sympathy for his wife and family who understandably were profoundly shocked.

Mr Metcalfe's suicide came nearly at the final meeting of the present board of governors. A new board was due to be elected the following week.

Two days later, there was an inquest at the Scarborough courthouse. Mr Reid, the clerk to the governors, stated that while the accounts of the workhouse were in order, there was a deficit of one- hundred pounds which was not paid into the treasury. The coroner was in no doubt this was the reason that unhinged Mr Metcalfe and most likely the reason for the suicide. A verdict of 'Suicide while temporary insane' was recorded.

*

Scarborough Gaol and Punishments

1845, Newborough Bar and Gaol. (Henry Barlow Carter)

Scarborough is a town known for its Castle yet since 1640 the town's Gaol was not situated there but in various places around the town.

In 1640, the town's criminal fraternity was placed in the prison in Newborough Bar where conditions were stated to be decrepit and horrendous.

Punishments against women were humiliating and barbaric, especially for those who conceived out of wedlock. In 1637 Ann Barry, a spinster from Scarborough, fell in love with Robert Thompson, a joiner from Beverley. He promised her numerous times that his intentions were honourable and that one day they would marry.

However, before this day came, Mary fell pregnant. The authorities soon became aware that Mary had committed this 'wicked and sinful act' and the bailiffs ordered that she should be punished for her sins. For this, the constable marched her to the east side of Longwestgate Street, where she would be stripped from the waist upwards, whipped and publicly humiliated through the 300 yards along the street until 'her body be bloodie'.

A similar fate happened to Margaret Marryall who like Ann Barry found herself pregnant. To punish her the authorities took her to the sands where she was stripped to the waist then put on either a 'thewe or carte' (the officer in charge had the choice of which one to use). An iron collar would be placed around a woman's neck with a rope attached to it at one end while the other end was fastened to a cart, in this manner, she would be paraded around the streets.

Another form of punishment was the thewe or 'Ducking stool' used as a deterrent for offenders such as 'witches, and prostitutes'. This stool was a sturdy wooden chair, in which the offender was strapped. A long rope would then suspend this chair, and the offender ducked into the water. The ducking stool in Scarborough was at the end of the old pier. The last time it was used was in 1795 on a Mrs Gamble. This stool can be seen today in the Rotunda Museum.

The punishment for the male fathering an illegitimate child was far more lenient and consisted of paying for the child until he or she was seven years old when the child would then be eligible to enter an apprenticeship. In the case of Ann Barry's lover, he was ordered to pay ten shillings to the county gaoler for 'lying in bed with the woman for more than one month.' For the upkeep of the child, he was ordered to pay sixteen pence per week until the child was seven years old when the child would then be eligible to enter an apprenticeship. He was also ordered to pay two pounds towards the binding of the boy's apprenticeship.

Margaret's lover received a more lenient order of eightpence a week until the child reached seven years old.

*

Debtors were by far the biggest proportion of 18th-century prisons, and Scarborough was no exception. Many a trader who had fallen on hard times was taken to court by their creditors, and if the person was unable to pay the court-ordered judgement, they were considered destitute and incarcerated until they either worked off their debts via hard-labour or secured outside funds to settle the judgement.

Scarborough reserved three cells for debtors in Newborough Gaol who would pay 3 pennies for a bed for the night. A 'lock-up' or 'drunk tank' was also provided to accommodate the inebriated and worse for wear, who were locked up until they sobered up.

Some cells were below ground and the cells no bigger than 9 feet square and 7 feet high. It would not be unusual to witness the emergence of a dirt-encrusted hand waving desperately through the pavement grates, pleading for bread and water.

By 1840 the Newborough Bar prison had fallen into profound disrepair so much so that the chaplain refused to give a service there because of the appalling conditions. The Yorkshire Gazette reported at the time that the chaplain had tried his best endeavours to 'remove the evils that exist', but the ramshackle conditions made repentance virtually impossible.

The Corporation agreed that a new prison was needed. In March 1842, The Old Gaol at Newborough Bar was sold by auction for one hundred guineas, in accordance with the plans to make room for a some much anticipated public improvements, which would comprise of a beautifully ornate arched (Folly) entrance into Scarborough, which was now becoming a fashionable, delightful watering place.

In May 1842, prisoners moved to the new gaol on Castle Road. The Town Council agreed not to demolish the old gaol until the beginning of 1843 as they decided that it would be inconvenient and injurious to residents and visitors just as the season was starting.

One of the last people to escape from Newborough Gaol was Miss Grace Robinson, who had gone to stay with Mrs Hutchinson at the Talbot Inn in Scarborough, and was apprehended for stealing sugar, a crime fully proved against her. She was committed to the sessions and incarcerated in Newborough Gaol. After only two days she affected her escape by pulling several bricks out from under the windows of her prison room and lowered herself down by her bedding to the yard below. She made her escape and was never seen again.

*

Interesting Inhabitants of Scarborough Gaol

John Hatfield (Public Domain)

One of Newborough Gaol's most notorious inmates was John Hatfield, who would later be known as 'The Keswick Swindler'. Hatfield was born in 1758 at Mortram in Longdale, Cheshire. As a teenager, he met a girl from a neighbouring farm who had been brought up to believe that she was a farmer's daughter, but her natural father was, in fact, the British Army General, Lord Robert Manners the 4th Duke of Rutland.

The Duke intended to give his daughter one thousand pounds, provided she married with his approval. The devious John Hatfield discovered this and immediately paid his respects to the lady representing himself as a young man of considerable expectations in the wholesale linen business. Manners perceiving the young man to be what he represented, gave his consent to the marriage immediately and the day after the marriage presented the bridegroom with a draft for fifteen hundred pounds. With this money, Hatfield lived the high life in London renting a house in Mayfair and making acquaintances in the right places. The money was soon spent, and Hatfield ran up massive debts which his father-in-law paid on the requirement that they left the country. The couple emigrated to America where they had three children. John Hatfield deserted his family and returned to London. The poor Mrs Hatfield died not long after, destitute and broken-hearted.

Hatfield returned to London, soon ran up enormous debts and eventually was imprisoned. The Duke once again came to his rescue and secured his release. Hatfield then toured the spa counties such as Bath and Leamington Spa.

In March 1792, he arrived in Scarborough without any attendants claiming to be on a fleeting visit from York where he had left his carriages and servants. The reason for his visit was to be proposed as the next MP for the Scarborough area, boasting that he was related to the Duke of Rutland through marriage. His manners were impeccable, and he called himself Major Hatfield, claiming to have fought in the conflict between England and America. On his arrival in Scarborough, he took up residence at the then principal inn of the town The New Inn, Newborough, which was kept by Mr William Stephens. Within a few days, Hatfield invited many members of the corporation and other well-known respectable members of the community to dinner. He apologised to them all for his humble appearance, and his conversation at dinner was cordial, always referring to his special relationship with his father-in-law The Duke of Rutland. Suspicions were soon raised when Hatfield cried openly when the fate of certain deceased Generals was mentioned. Hatfield claimed that they were close personal friends of his.

Three weeks after his arrival the host of the New Inn Mr Stephens asked Hatfield for a sum of thirty pounds towards his account. Hadfield readily offered a banker's draft on his bank in town, this draft was not accepted and not paid.

Consequently, his actions raised suspicion and the authenticity of Hatfield's 'tales were disputed. Mr Stephens called the police and Hatfield was arrested for the tavern debt on 27th April 1792. Hatfield claimed it was all a mistake and that everything would be settled soon, but that didn't happen. Hatfield was unable to procure bail. In the meantime, a Mr Joseph Hamilton of London sent a detainer to Scarborough court claiming a debt Hatfield had with him amounting to 80 guineas. Hatfield was found guilty and sent to Scarborough Gaol for a term of seven years.

During his confinement Hatfield received many vicissitudes from unknown sources- several remittances exceeded his debts. However, he relied on the basic allowance he received from the gaol, except when mistaken benevolence occasionally interposed. In one instance, he received by sale of some property belonging to his wife a sum of one hundred and eighty pounds and at the same time revealed that he had been promoted to the rank of Lieutenant Colonel and applied to the gaol to allow the Militia Band to play to him on this happy event.

Every half year Hatfield dared to request the attendance of a magistrate to swear an affidavit to obtain half-pay as Major or Lieutenant Hatfield. On other occasions impatient with his confinement he would write supplicant or threatening letters to the Bailiffs of Scarborough criticising the dilapidated state of the gaol. On the door of his cell, he inscribed the words 'Here lies interred John Hatfield'. He even wrote a 'Guide anonymously to Scarborough' in which he condemned the Gaol extensively.

These are his words on his impression of the prison;

Gaoler's House.   Old Prison,
NEWBROUGH BAR AS IT APPEARED IN 1646.

'The building is a public nuisance, as it spoils the entrance to the town. Its interior is a disgrace to the country. What are the readers' feelings on being told that prisoners confined for debt are kept continually locked upstairs? That woman, the only keepers have the yard entirely to themselves for washing linen of strangers who come to the Spa. Alas, this is all too true, and within the last five years, every poor wretch was kept constantly locked in his room, not even allowed a passage to walk in, which is only 4 feet wide, and shortened nearly one half by a large room being taken off (much the best room in the prison) for the exclusive use of its keepers!

For the honour of humanity, and the reputation of Scarborough, let us hope for a speedy and effectual remedy be found for such gross violations of every decent principle.

There is not any sort of Gaol allowance the author has been informed of good authority. Similar abuses had long been a disgrace to the prison for debtors in Dover Castle, but that last summer (1796) some alterations were made for the accommodation of the unhappy persons confined there. Particularly, that a court has enclosed about 50 ft. in length, where they are in future to enjoy the long-denied privilege of a promenade, so essential to the health and so great an alleviation to the confinement of the prisoner.'

At the end of eight years, he obtained his discharge, aided with the help of a Miss Michelli Nation, a young lady who was staying in Newborough opposite the prison for the spa season. The young lady was instantly smitten with this handsome man. Hatfield is reported to have said at the time.

'We gazed at each other through the bars of the Gaol as if we were already lovers. Every day we looked at each other at the same time for seven years. The only time she was absent was when she went to London to plead my case or down to Devonshire for more funds from her fortune to procure my release.'

Hatfield was released from Gaol at ten o'clock in the evening of Saturday 12th September. At his request, he asked to stay one night longer. The following morning, he was released, then he and Miss Nation went straight to St Mary's church in Scarborough and were married by special licence. Hatfield and his second wife left Scarborough for Devonshire. The couple had two children, but Hatfield deserted his wife two years later.

Predictably, this was not the end of the notorious Hatfield, he continued his pretension and antics around the country, eventually marrying for the third time to an unsuspecting young girl in Buttermere known locally as 'the Beauty of Buttermere'. Hatfield was going under the name of The Honourable Alexander Augustus Hope. Hatfield was eventually caught and sentenced to death for Forgery and Bigamy. Hatfield was executed on 3rd September 1803 in front of a large crowd.

*

Castle Road Gaol

Credit Paul Thomas

Conditions at the new jail were only marginally better than that at Newborough. Security was lacking, and the Prison Governors were concerned about the number of escapees which continued to be a problem for the remainder of the prison's existence. Furthermore, although the prison was only twenty years old, it did not fit the guidelines of the new Prisons Act of 1865, which stipulated that better accommodation was to be provided for long-term inmates.

Consequently, the council had to find alternative land for the building of a new prison.

Many types of crimes came before the courthouse. One of the most common cases amongst women was the charge of 'concealment of a child'. The Victorians placed great emphasis on the bonds of marriage which were considered the social norm and anyone deviating from this would bring great shame on themselves and their families. Women who found themselves in the position of carrying a 'bastard child' would often do anything to conceal their pregnancy and the birth of a child. One such case came before Justice Creswell at the Courthouse in July 1846. Martha Duck aged 29 was charged with the concealment of a child and exposing this male infant to the cold with the intent to murder the said child, a charge Martha strongly denied. A witness, Mr William Wilson from Scarborough, had seen the prisoner walking around the field for some time, he then saw her go into a barn, and when she came out, she was carrying a bundle which she left behind a bush. Mr Wilson spoke to Martha who appeared to be in the family way.

Another witness, a Mr Henry Richmond, stated that later the same day he heard a baby crying and found a baby boy behind the bush covered in grass and broad leaves. The place he saw the child had no footpath and was not an accessible route. The child was not clean and had blood on it. Mr Richmond wrapped the child in his coat and took it to Jane Ireland of Scalby Mills.

Mrs Ireland gave evidence, saying that the child was new-born and that the navel string was not tied. She gave it a little gin and water and gave it to another woman who suckled it. The child was placed in the care of the Scarborough Union Workhouse. Mr Dunkerley, the workhouse master, said the child was still alive but suffered from fits for a long time after its arrival in his facility.

The prisoner denied that she was the child's mother and said that she had not had a child for ten or eleven years. However, a medical examination was ordered by the court, and Martha eventually admitted that she was the child's mother. Lucky for Martha a medical man, Mr Richard Cross, empathised with her situation and pleaded Martha's case saying that he grieved for her position. Martha was found guilty, but considering the doctor's comments, the judge deferred any sentence.

Just one week before the prison was due to close, Mr Edgar who was serving a sentence of eighteen months for passing counterfeit coins was the last recorded prisoner to escape from the Castle Road jail. He did this by removing the mortar to the lock of his cell with a palette knife; it appears that another prisoner probably helped him and that they had little difficulty.

The jail on Castle Road closed as a prison in 1866 but continued as a courthouse and police station before closure in 1971.

*

Dean Road Prison

Credit Deborah Bradley

Castle Road Prison was only twenty years old, but it failed to meet the expectations and standards of the Prison Act 1865, which stipulated that long-term prisoners should receive better accommodation. A new prison was needed, and suitable land was found in Penny Black Lane owned by the solicitor Mr Edward S Donner and the trustees of the late brewer Mr E D Nesfield. The prison was designed by the architect William Baldwin Stewart with gothic arches, four turrets and arrow slits. The foundation stone for the new jail was laid on 24th October 1865 by the Mayor Mr Ambrose Gibson and shortly after a rooftop supper was held at the Prince of Wales Hotel for 300 dignified guests.

For the building of the prison, the corporation obtained a mortgage of fourteen thousand pounds (including additions) and the new jail opened in October 1866. Twenty-two males and twenty-two female prisoners were transferred from Castle Road Gaol. There were thirty-six cells built on three floors. Twelve to each floor, six on each side. The whitewashed walls were two feet thick. Over the time that the prison was operational, it had favourable reports from the Prison Inspector and was one of the best prisons in the country.

Unfortunately, under Viscount Cross's prison reform bill, 'The Prison Act 1877' announced that the operation of all prisons in the United Kingdom was to be centralised and transferred away from local authorities giving ultimate power over the running of prisons to the Home Office. Despite Scarborough's model prison only being open eleven years, the prison had to obey the new rules, and in July 1878 it closed.

A few years later a deputation from Scarborough Corporation called upon the Home Secretary requesting that Scarborough is reopened based on the costs of transportation of prisoners to either Hull or York Castle. The petition fell on deaf ears. Therefore, the corporation remained liable for the repayment of the mortgage which at the time of closure was ten-thousand two hundred and fifty pounds and was also required to pay into the exchequer under the new Prison Act just over two-thousand was to enable them to keep possession of their property. In addition to this burden, they were also incurring an annual expense of one-hundred and fifty pounds for the conveying of prisoners. It made no sense.

The prison stood empty for many years. Over time it has been used as a dog-pound, a council yard for the council's engineering department. At one time there was the talk of the prison been reformed into a hotel. Grade 2 listed building status was granted to the prison in 1985. A few years ago, it featured in a television programme entitled 'Banged up,' when the then Home Secretary David Plunkett acted as the Head of the Parole Board.

*

There have been some interesting people come through the gates of this model prison, and others were impatient and not wanting to finish their sentence they went over the wall. Here are just a few stories of some of the gaol's interesting inmates.

In 1866, A disreputable thief whose real name was William Jobling but who was known in Scarborough as Walter Scott was in Scarborough Gaol on a charge of stealing jewellery from a Mr Walter Mellor MP from a lodging house in Scarborough. On the night in question, all the prisoners were checked, and all found to be present, but as daylight dawned it soon became apparent that Walter Scott was missing, and the way he escaped quickly became apparent.

Each cell had a gaslight, water tap and ventilators. Scott escaped by climbing through a ventilator duct in his cell. To do this, he suspended a piece of steel over the gaslight making a turnscrew from it; he then unscrewed an iron plate which covered the water-pipes, then he removed the ventilator (which was under the window) together with the surrounding bricks allowing him to crawl through. He then threw his blankets out, then by a self-made neck brace he swung his body from the hole and grabbing the fall-pipe he successfully descended three floors to the ground. He landed in a large yard. He then tore up his blankets, tying them together to make a rope; at the end of this rope, he made a bag and put a couple of bricks in it and swung it over the wall. Fortunately for Scott, in this yard was some old bedstead and clothes-post which Scott used as scaffolding. He climbed over the wall and ran off into the fields. Many efforts were made to recapture Scott, including mounted police, telegraph and photography. Unfortunately, all to no avail.

Jobling spent two years on the run before a tip-off led the police to a house in Gateshead, where the police found Jobling sitting in a chair quietly smoking a cigar. Despite putting up a fight, the prisoner was soon arrested and transported back to Scarborough where he was finally sentenced for the thefts and for escaping from custody. When arrested, the police discovered a paper in his possession which showed plans to break into Lambeth Castle and other prestigious houses.

*

Two Female Imposters of the Century

Women were just as disreputable. Two women arrived in Scarborough in September 1869 and stayed one night at the Talbot Hotel. The ladies were well-to-do, well educated, cheerful and had an air of confidence and aristocracy about them. The ladies were not over-enamoured with the room in the hotel and wanted somewhere better and more suitable. The next day they moved to the Castle Hotel. Still, they remained unhappy and asked to be recommended to some first-class lodgings as they were ladies and accustomed to the finer things in life. They complained of having to mix with 'vulgar' people at the Castle Hotel, and they considered it very off-putting. They explained that their page boy would be joining them soon. For this extra accommodation, they agreed to pay Mrs Brady of 7 Granby Place an extra ten pounds a month. Mrs Brady found the ladies a house, but again they were not happy saying the house was still not to their standard. The ladies asked her to take them to a Villa on South-Cliff for a rental of two-hundred pounds a year.

The younger female told Mrs Brady that she was a ward of Chancery and that in a few days she would receive a large sum of money bequeathed to her, and asked Mrs Brady which one of the Scarborough Banks would be best to deposit an amount of two- thousand pounds? She also told the story of how she was related to Robert the Bruce, and that she had an interest in estates in Jamaica.

After convincing many of their wealth, the ladies went on a shopping spree, buying goods on credit from all the best tradesmen and jewellers in town including a significant debt to Marshall & Snelgrove.

The younger woman again said that her trustee was a physician to the Queen and that he was coming to Scarborough to get her mother's signature on a document. She again asked Mrs Brady is she could get good lodgings for the trustee of up to seven guineas a week. On the day the trustee was due to arrive the younger woman produced a velvet dress, which she said did not fit and that she needed to take it for alterations.

The two ladies then went about their business and were never seen or heard from again. The ladies always left a trunk behind in their room to give the impression that they would be returning. However, on opening the trunk people would find that it filled with nothing more than bricks and sawdust.

A short time later the Head Constable of Scarborough received a telegram advising that these two women who were in fact sisters had spent the last twenty-five years travelling the country swindling people out of money. The Head Constable was determined to capture these women. He devised a plan and contacted the ladies' brother who agreed to cooperate with the police. The brother Dr Trutch told the police that the women's legacy was due soon and which post office the sisters would be at to collect it. The police went undercover, and soon the elder sister came in dressed in the height of fashion.

Taking the woman by surprise, the officer said, 'Good morning Miss Trutch.' Startled, the woman turned around and spoke to the officer.

'Do you know you who you are talking to?' to which the officer sternly replied.

'Yes.'

The lady then knew she had been caught and said.

'You fool! Hold your noise, we are being watched. Come home with me, and I will see what I can do.'

The officer escorted Miss Trutch to her lodgings where her younger sister was sleeping. The elder sister began to laugh uncontrollably at the constable.

'You thought you did us very cleverly at Manchester, but I had a parcel of jewellery concealed in the pocket of my petticoat. We sold them and swiftly took the train back to Birmingham.'

Both women were arrested and placed in handcuffs, and as they sat in the police car to be transported back to Scarborough to stand trial, they were pelted with eggs by some of the tradesmen they had conned.

The sisters received a sentence of eight months in prison. The eldest sister Mary died of a heart-attack in Dean Road Gaol in 1870.

The story doesn't end there though. Now known as the Torquay swindler the younger sister continued in her role using many assumed names. She told the unsuspecting traders that she had a legacy of one-thousand pounds from her departed sister. She was eventually arrested in Bath under the name of Miss Gledhill, but not before she had swindled many more shopkeepers out of their stock.

*

Schools & Literary Institutions

The Education Act of 1880 made education compulsory for all children up to the age of ten and increased to thirteen from 1896.

Before this, Scarborough had a scattering of private and church funded schools.

In 1827, there was an infant school on St Sepulchre Street, and a national school for girls erected in 1836 directly opposite the Amicable Society. The boys' school erected a year later situated at the top of Queen Street. An infant school opened in 1845 in Tuthill near St Thomas Chapel for sixty children, formed to meet the educational needs of the seafaring community.

There were various religious societies with school rooms such as the Bible Society and the Tract Society which was at 49 Newborough Street.

The Lancastrian School built-in 1810 in a field at the end of Rope Walk leading up to St Mary's church held four hundred children and was funded by subscriptions.

The date of the founding of a grammar school in Scarborough is unknown and reportedly goes back to medieval times with a mention of a headmaster named Hugh Rasen one of the town's bailiffs and an MP for the area in 1422 (Scarborough News, 2013). The school most likely had its origins in the dissolution of the Carmelite convent, as records from 1597 show that the high school had twenty pupils each paying a subscription. In 1684, the school ceased to be in the grips of the convent, and in the same year, town bailiff Francis Thompson gave one hundred pounds for the use of the school. Furthermore, the interest from this sum was intended for supplying books for the school. However, instead, the vicar used the funds for his personal use as he considered himself 'entitled' as he was the lecturer! (Barker)

St Martin's Grammar merged with the Municipal School of Westwood which were previously rival schools from opposite sides of the town. Fortunately, the amalgamation was a success, and both sides of the valley worked together in perfect harmony.

The ladies had a school of industry, which prepared them for employment in domestic service, and other household duties.

Schools & Literary Institutions

Paradise House Graham Sea Training School

Paradise house, formerly known as Tindall House, and the birthplace of Sir George Cayley is a large house overlooking the town located just underneath the Castle. Colonel CC Graham, Scarborough's then Lord Mayor, purchased the house in 1918 and gave the property to the town for setting up England's first sea-training school where boys received training in all aspects of the sea.

Practical training in the engineering shop in 1921

The school had strong links with the Navy who offered advice and training to the cadets. The school bought a schooner named after Colonel Graham's daughter, Maisie, unfortunately, Col Graham's son was killed in action in the First World War.

The school was taken over by the North Riding in 1944, and in the 1970s the school closed. In 1973 it became part of the boys' high school. The property is now private flats.

*

Part Two Scarborough Old Town

Aubrough Gate.

The ancient town of Scarborough was protected by a wall confined within narrow limits. The first inhabitants of the town were most likely fishermen scattered around the seashore. These walls had gates or Bars which were used to control the people entering in and out of the town. The gates in the town were at Auborough Bar, Newborough Bar, West Sandgate, East Sandgate and Barbican Gate at the Castle. The building of the Castle and subsequently the Church of St Mary's would invite many artisans and labourers to the town leading to an increase in the population.

The town wall and the moat circled the town from the harbour to Bar Street to the Castle. The historian Leland said of Scarborough's two gates leading into the town by land: 'Newburg Gate – meatley good, and

Aldeburg Gate – very base.' He also said: 'The town is waulled a little with ston, but most with ditches and waulles of yerth.'

It is not known when the walls of the old town crumbled away. Much of the stone was used to build houses in Aldborough Street and the lower end of Newborough. The mediaeval New Borough spread westwards as far as is now Huntriss Row, where the new moat began. This moat passed under the Newborough gates and continued behind St Thomas Hospital, then north-east onto Awborough Gate.

Before the opening of the Cliff Bridge, the town of Scarborough was nestled down towards the harbour, with no population except for a few houses on the North Shore.

The South Cliff was a vast desolate waste with one single white cottage built on the slope. As the town expanded in respectability and opulence, the town gradually descended the hill, north and west. Although Scarborough had been an up and coming holiday resort, it was still very quiet in winter with one coach between Scarborough and York each day. The Royal Mail left York for Scarborough and returned every evening with four passengers outside and four inside. In the summer months, three or four stagecoaches were travelling to Scarborough, which would hold ten people outside and four inside. Until the year 1722, the only road for carriages from the town to the seashore was through Merchants Row and West Sandgate where nobility passed.

Around this time Mr John Bland, a Quaker merchant undertook to make at his own expense, a 'horse-way' down the cliff to the sands and to pave the same from the top to the bottom, and to build a substantial staithe or wall facing the sea, and the corporation was to pay him eighty-five pounds on account. John Bland fulfilled this operation and completed it also to accommodate carriages. Hence this area still retains the name of its creator: Bland's Cliff.

*

Water Conduits

The middle conduit credit Scarborough Friends Reunited. (Facebook).

The town's water supply was in three conduits around the town. Low conduit, which was on Princess Square, a Middle conduit which was in Market Hall and Upper or Great Conduit which was on Newborough. This system lasted for over seven hundred years. Each household was required to provide a labouring man to dig up and relay the conduit pipes running from Falsgrave to Newborough or pay 6d for 'Sayd Worke'.

There was also a fine of one shilling for anyone who let his horse or beast drink from out of any of the conduits and the same for anyone who washed clothes or cleaned vessels within six yards of them. There were also complaints that the brewers were using the middle conduit far too much, so as a precaution the town bellman covered and locked it with a trapdoor between the hours of 6 pm and 6 am to prevent them using it.

By 1845, the people were tired of having to wait their turn at the water conduits and wanted a more convenient way to collect their water. Subsequently, a company was formed to supply the town with plentiful stock. A spring at Cayton Bay, previously used as an old corn- mill which had attached to it a working spring was put into service. A consortium of local businessmen purchased the mill and its spring, and a pumping engine installed capable of pumping 400,000 gallons. In 1853, another similar engine capable of a further 650,000 gallons a day was installed. Thirty years after, the company sank a well and put down a pumping plant at Osgoodby. By 1878, the corporation realised that there was money in water, and set about discrediting the local private water companies and insisted on a referendum, the corporation declared all no-votes in their favour and unsurprisingly, the corporation won the vote. Like the rest of the country, the water supply was more-or-less untreated until 1913 when filters were fitted at Irton ensuring best quality water for all.

Street Cleaning & Lights

In 1775, and again in 1805 an Act of Parliament was obtained for paving lighting and cleansing the streets. In 1810 by voluntary subscriptions, lamps for lighting the streets were erected, later the maintenance of these lights and afterwards the system was transferred to the commissioners under the Improvement Act. Residents of the borough were expected to keep the area in front and behind their houses clean and ensure gutters were cleaned regularly, no offal, dung, dirt, manure or rubbish – and no wandering pigs!

In 1893, the practice of lighting the town with gas lamps became inadequate and the lighting of the streets irregular, the time came to consider lighting the streets with electric light. The contract for the gas company rescinded once their present contract came to an end, and electricity came to the streets of Scarborough for the first time in 1882 when the council applied for a motion to light the town with electricity, six private companies applied but the corporation did not want to encourage a monopoly. Therefore, the Scarborough Electric Light Company was the company selected.

Markets & Fairs

Like many other towns across the country, markets were an integral part of life and essential importance to commerce and Scarborough was no exception. However, there had been a rivalry for many years between the markets of Scarborough and Seamer, so litigation followed.

In the year 1181, King Henry II gave to the burgesses of the town of Scarborough permission to hold a market, the same as the liberties and customs of that of York citizens. The right for Seamer to hold a market was granted by Richard II to Henry Earl of Northumberland in the year 1383, which was held for seven days following the feast of St Martin, together with a weekly market. However, this grant came with the exception that if 'it should be found injurious to the neighbouring markets and fairs, then it must be stopped.' Therefore, a market was suppressed and not held in Seamer until 1577 when Sir Henry Gate, Knight and proprietor of Seamer procured an exemplification of Richard II's charter.

Hence, Scarborough was not happy, and the bailiffs and burgesses of Scarborough protested and commenced proceedings at the Queen's Bench for the suppression of Seamer Market. Declaring that this market was 'injurious' to Scarborough, and that trade was suffering, citing that before Seamer there were eight bakers at Scarborough, but now only 4. The same with butchers and drapers and that the overall quality of goods sold on the market had decreased. Also, the long-established Scarborough Market and previous markets at Filey, Sherbourne and Brompton had been suppressed in favour of Scarborough and that the town paid a farm rent of ninety-one pounds to the crown raised by gablage, corn-tolls and the rent of mills. In defence, the residents of the adjoining areas testified that Seamer market was better stocked and that the roads to Scarborough were 'evil and miry' in winter. After many years of litigation amounting to 2000/- judgement was given in favour of Scarborough market and the market at Seamer was suppressed. However, many of the hierarchy at Scarborough did not believe that Seamer had, in fact, stopped the market and they were still doing on under the guise of a 'gathering or a meeting' so Scarborough petitioned again. The suspension at Seamer was reaffirmed and Sir Henry Gate given a stern warning, after continual postponements the market was finally suppressed in Seamer in 1612.

Scarborough market then increased, and there were various markets around the town, these are a few.

Weekly markets were held twice a week on Saturdays and Thursdays. Saturday Market held in Princess Street (Formerly Nether Westgate), and Thursday market was in Newborough Street and sold earthenware, pots and pans etc.

The ancient market cross was at Low Conduit, West Sandgate at the north corner. This cross is frequently mentioned in the corporation records as 'Butter Cross' and was one of the stations where the municipal authorities made public proclamations.

Apple Market

Held in King Street until 1880.

Beast Market

Formerly held in Queen Street but removed to Wrea Lane near where the abattoir was then situated. This market attracted farmers from far and wide and held two times a year on Holy Thursday and Martinmas day. The meat market held in St Helen's Square in the Old Shambles was demolished to make way for the new market hall built on this same site in 1853.

The earliest account of a market in Scarborough is around 1181, most likely held near the rope-walk north of Toller gate.

For the security of dealings, contracts were witnessed in the presence of an officer appointed for that purpose by the lord of the market, and for which he would receive a small remuneration known as 'a market toll'.

Cloth Market

Attended by people from the manufacturing districts who had cloth to buy and sell. Clothiers held out at the south end of Queen Street, and their goods were displayed in a double row of stalls, one row at each end of the street.

In Edward VI's reign, the fish market was first held on the sands. Trade seems to have been quite extensive, with sheepskins and wool being essential items. Besides the merchants selling their wares, there were carpenters, joiners, glove-makers, blacksmiths, weavers, potters and painters. The old town must have been quite a hive of industry, in addition to traditional fishing and boatbuilding.

The Blue Stone & The Butter Cross

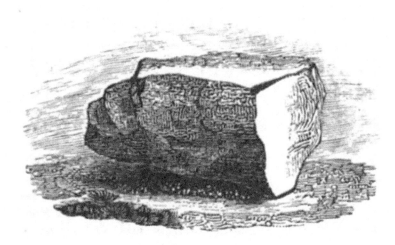

THE BLUE STONE.

The Rotunda Museum holds the original blue stone (Basalt). This stone is where many a bargain was ratified. It was at one time located at the north end of High Toller Gate on the road to St Mary's Church and held in the wall in this area. People were expected to pay for goods bought upon the stone and witnessed by another.

The Market Cross

Credit Scarborough Old Photos. Facebook Group.

The earliest known reference to the Market Cross or the Butter Cross is in 1395 and it is understood to have formed part of the old borough in the 1200s.

This ancient cross stood proudly on the site of the once-thriving Saturday Market overlooked by St Mary's Church in the middle of what was once Conduit Street, in front of Ye Old Brass Tap pub, which was then a focal point for many a meeting. Cole in his history of Scarborough writes about the Market Cross. 'The market was held upon the sands in the reign of Edward VI. It was held in other parts of town and the remains of a very ancient market cross are still standing.' The Market Cross was moved to a 'more conspicuous position' in 1904.

Scarborough Builds a 'New Market'.

In 1851 notice was given by Scarborough Corporation of their intention to apply to Parliament for the establishment of a new market for the sale of butcher's meat, poultry, fish, butter, cheese, vegetables, corn-hay, and other provisions goods and wares merchandise and commodities. For the construction of the market, the corporation intended to sell shares and raise a mortgage. They petitioned to erect a market with suitable buildings such as shops, sheds, and weighing machines situated near Carr Street, St Helen's Square. The Corporation also presented plans to block up the passages and thoroughfares called The Shambles and Bennetts yards and all other courts and passages near to the intended site.

Furthermore, the Corporation asked for the removal of the public water conduit and the public fountain and weighing house in St Helen's Square. The bill received Royal assent on its third reading in the House of Lords, and building work commenced soon after.

In 1852 the company advertised for builders.

SCARBOROUGH MARKET HALL.

THE DIRECTORS of the SCARBOROUGH PUBLIC MARKET COMPANY are prepared to receive TENDERS for the execution of the MASONRY, BRICKWORK, SLATERS', IRON-FOUNDERS', CARPENTERS', JOINERS', PAINTERS', PLUMBERS', and GLAZIERS' WORK, required in the ERECTION of their NEW MARKET HALL, in Saint Helen's Square, in the Borough of Scarborough, and County of York.

The Drawings and Specifications may be seen at the Architect's Office, in the Savings' Bank, in Scarborough, on and after TUESDAY, the 26th Day of October instant, from TEN o'Clock a.m., to FOUR o'Clock p.m.

Sealed Tenders must be sent to me, endorsed " Scarborough Market Hall," " Tender for Works," on or before TUESDAY, the 9th Day of November next, at TEN o'Clock in the Forenoon.

Sureties will be required for the due performance of the respective Contracts.

Lithographed Copies of the Quantities will be furnished.

The Directors do not bind themselves to accept the Lowest Tenders.

By Order,

SAMUEL BAILEY,

October 18th, 1852.   Secretary.

In December 1921, the court's Brewster sessions heard an application from licensee Mr Tasker Hart. Mr Hart represented seven licensed premises in the area namely, The Shakespeare, Star, Talbot, George, Balmoral, Queens Head and the Plough. The licensee's wanted to be allowed to open their premises on a Thursday afternoon – Market day.

The gentlemen argued that there was a need for extra facilities and that farmers did their business around mid-afternoon and that refreshments were needed. They also claimed that Scarborough Market had been adversely affected in comparison to other market towns where licensing laws had been relaxed to accommodate farmers and tradesmen.

After a lengthy hearing, the chairman Mr WS Rowntree said that the magistrates were not satisfied that the need was necessary and refused the application.

Scarborough 'Jabbers' Fair

WikiCommons

The annual fair was held on 12th August when people gathered from all over the country and pitched their tents on Merchants Row and Palace Hill and the south-east of the town. The Fair was a big event and was opened in a grand-traditional style by the town officials, musicians, jesters and followers who all paraded through the streets. A bell rang to signify the opening of the fair, it was illegal for a sale to commence before the bell and no male or female could buy any goods, or fish or herring unless it was after the ringing of the bell, on land, in the market and after the ship had anchored in the port. Furthermore, the burgesses of Scarborough had the right to be served first.

Scarborough Fair was well known, and merchants from as far away as Ghent and the Baltic ports would be present. Many items were sold here from woollen cloth from Flanders and other German and foreign wares. After the bell was sounded minstrels and jugglers in colourful suits would declare the market open. Music Bands and crowds of men, women and children would make a ground procession, some of them on horseback. Even the horses were decorated with flowers as were the hats of the riders. The streets of Scarborough were decorated, and a town crier would welcome people to the famous fair. During the opening of the Fair, tolls were collected, and anyone entering the town from other places would have to pay the toll at the gate, and the toll would be dependent on the number of horses or vehicles the trader had. The opening ceremony started with a poem;

'Lords, gentlemen, and loons.
You're welcome to our toons
Until Saint Michaelmas day
But Tolls and customs pay
Taken notice evericke one
This fair be kept till set of sun
No sort of food. I rede ye sell
But what will fit the body well
No sort of goods I rede ye vend
Unless their worth ye first commend
And also, all be found to please
On pain of stocks and a little ease
And buyers all that common here
The wanted dues and tolls shall clear
Now may you sport and play I wis
And all things do, but nowt amiss
So quick your booths and tents prepare
And welcome strangers to the Fair
God save the King, and the worshipped Bailiff's

This annual Fair continued until 1788 when owing to competition from neighbouring Seamer it fell into disrepute.

Entertainment

The Assembly Rooms, Lodging Rooms, Long Room Street

Old Assembly Rooms Sandside. (Joseph Newington Carter 1871)

Dukes and gentry were plentiful in Scarborough in the early 1700s who frequented the Longroom, the coffee house and the bookshop. To accommodate the elite Long Room Street, Queen Street and Newborough were rebuilt to city standards, and in the 1760s came the building of the lodging houses on the cliff.

The summer season started in July and was a short one. The drinking room at the Spaw and the paths around it were dirty, one visitor describing Scarborough as 'A dirty ill built and very badly paved town.' Assembly rooms were popular and were gathering places for upper-class men and women in the 18th and 19th centuries. Scarborough had two.

One on Low Westgate Street was old and became less popular and subsequently closed and turned into tenements. The other Assembly room was on Long Room Street (St Nicholas Street) which together with Queen Street had large stones and posts, this area was commonly referred to as 'Scarborough's Pall Mall'. Mr Donner ran the Long Room (which would later become the Royal Hotel) with balls and dancing most nights where gentlemen paid only one-shilling each to dance.

At one end was a gallery for musicians and side rooms with card tables. Sumptuous dinners were helped at 2 pm each day. Subscriptions were five shillings each for both gentlemen and ladies. Dinners consisted of 10 courses with a glass of spaw water mixed with wine. There would be an afternoon play usually by a Mr Keregan.

The rooms at the Long Room were elegant and suited people of the most exquisite fashion and taste. The rules of the rooms were as follows. The programme for Wednesday night seems most interesting.

Rules of The Rooms

I.

The subscription to the Rooms for the season is 11s.

II.

The dress nights are Mondays and Fridays on which nights non-subscribers pay 5s each.

III.

Wednesday is an undress night, on which non-subscribers pay the same.

IV.

Every gentleman who dances pays 2s for himself and partner towards the music.

V.

Every lady or gentleman who drinks tea pay 1s.

Besides such amusements as hunting, shooting, and coursing which gentleman was accustomed to in the neighbourhood. There were also available trips around the glorious bay, and of course fishing.

Mr Donner operated these well-known premises on Long Room Street for some considerable time often advertising that his premises were the only one in town that commanded a full view of the sea and that his accommodation afforded every convenience not only as a boarding house but also to private families and parties.

However, Mr Donner was ageing, and in 1837 he placed an advert in the local paper announcing that he wished to retire and that he was looking for either a purchaser or tenant on moderate terms. Just when it seemed that Scarborough had lost its social centre a young man named John Fairgrey Sharpin, aged only 24 was determined to fill that social void. Mr Sharpin was so charmed with the beauty of Scarborough he was resolute to make it his home.

He answered this advert and soon turned the Royal Hotel into one of the most celebrated venues in the country.

SCARBRO'

HOTEL, LONG-ROOM-STREET.

Mr DONNER respectfully informs his friends and the public, that this long-established House and the only Hotel in Scarbro' commanding an uninterrupted view of the sea, is open for the reception of visitors, having been considerably improved.

As Mr Donner proposes retiring from the business, he is disposed to treat with a purchaser or tenant upon moderate terms.

All letters to be post-paid. June 1837.

*

Sharpin was a capable young man who, within ten years, would become the youngest Town Mayor in England. He bought and demolished two buildings at the Westborough end of Huntriss Row (Now Pizza Hut) and erected a new building, which became Scarborough's Assembly Rooms. These rooms opened in June 1857; the new venue provided a more extensive range of entertainment and catered for concerts, billiards, the arts and a restaurant.

These advertisements show what was on the bill at the time.

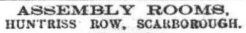

ASSEMBLY ROOMS,
HUNTRISS ROW, SCARBOROUGH.

FIFTH WEEK OF

SURPRISES & DISGUISES

**The most instructive and entertaining
Musical Novelty of the present day.**
(See the opinions of the Press.)

SURPRISES AND DISGUISES,
Or Popular Peculiarities.

A ROMANTIC Rhapsody most romantically re-
lated by Mr. W. H. Eburne, and Miss
Emmeline Martyn, on Monday, Sept. 6th,
and each Evening during the week—commencing at
a Quarter past Eight, precisely.
The Doors will be open at a Quarter to Eight.
Pianiste.— Miss Lizzie Parry.
Solos on the Guitar, Violin, and Pianoforte, by
Miss Emmeline Martyn. Songs, humorous and
sentimental, by Mr. W. H. Eburne. Duets, by the
Artistes, and sixteen different characters personised
New Music and change of Programme each Evening.

Two Grand Morning Performances,
Combined with the splendid **Exhibition** of
Paintings, on Monday, September the 6th and
Wednesday, the 8th. Tickets to be had of Mr.
Bowman, at the Assembly Rooms, which will admit
to the Exhibition of Paintings from 10 to 1, and to
the Morning Performance of **Surprises and
Disguises,** commencing at Two o'clock precisely.
The Room will be arranged for Promenade during
Exhibition and as a Concert Room for the Musical
Entertainment.
Prices, 2s.; 1s.; and Gallery, 6d.; Stalls, numbered
2s. 6d.

The esteemed author Charles Dickens, who was already a literary figure and a well-known celebrity, gave two readings here in the year 1858. Here is the advertisement for the reading from Little Dombey and A Christmas Carol.

MR. CHARLES DICKENS

Will read at the

ASSEMBLY ROOMS, SCARBOROUGH,

ON Monday Afternoon, September 13th, at Three o'clock, the Story of **Little Dombey.** On Monday Evening, September 13th, at Eight o'clock. his **Christmas Carol.**

Places for each Reading :—Stalls, (numbered and reserved,) Five Shillings ; Area, Half-a-Crown ; Gallery, One Shilling. Tickets to be had of Mr. Edward Morton, at the Assembly Rooms, where a Plan of the Stalls may be seen. Each Reading will last two hours.

St. Nicholas Gate (Long Room Street – St Nicholas Street)

Long Room Street initially called St Nicholas Gate changed its name as its popularity increased. This area was the social emporium of the town and is where elegant purpose-built lodging houses were located including Wood's Lodgings where Anne Bronte stayed. Rooms were a similar price to those at Bath: 10 shillings a week including towels, sheets and table linen with servants' rooms at half-price. These houses were later demolished to make way for the building of The Grand Hotel.

Anne Bronte

Wood's Lodgings 1860. (Tony Amers)

Anne Bronte, the youngest of the Bronte literary family, is known for the novels Agnes Grey (1847), The Tenant of Wildfell Hall (1848), and her poetry. Anne loved Scarborough especially the sea which she watched from the windows of Wood's Lodgings on Long Room Street. Like her sister Emily before her and many others in the country, Anne contracted tuberculosis, the dreaded scourge of consumption. Anne grew weaker and knew there was little hope, and against her family's wishes, she persuaded her friend Ellen Nussey to accompany her to Scarborough, insisting that a change of air would be beneficial for her health. Anne's sister Charlotte had reservations and tried to stop her sister from travelling to Scarborough. However, she eventually respected her sister's wishes and joined Anne and her friend on what was to be her sister's final journey.

The women travelled to Scarborough by train and stopped overnight in York so that Anne could visit York Minster. Anne was very weak and when she reached number 2 The Cliffe known as 'Wood's Lodgings' a doctor was called. Her diagnosis was not good, and the doctor proclaimed that death was close. Anne took the news gracefully and sought solace in prayer. She died on 28th May 1849.

Charlotte wanted Anne's funeral to be at Scarborough's parish church of St Mary, but due to renovations, this was not possible. However, Anne's final resting place is in St Mary's churchyard overlooking the sea she loved so much. Charlotte arranged for a headstone made from Cloughton stone for her sister depicting an urn draped over two books. On the stone was a simple inscription;

'Here lie the remains of Anne Bronte, daughter of the Rev. P. Bronte, Incumbent of Haworth, Yorkshire. She died on 28 May 1849.' However, when Charlotte returned to visit the grave, she was shocked to see that there were five errors on Anne's headstone, one of them gave her age as 28 when she died when in fact, she was 29. This was an error which wasn't corrected until 164 years after her death. One of the other mistakes was the spelling lies instead of lie, and there is no record of what the other three were.

Initially, iron railings protected Anne's grave, but over the years this corroded, with no family to tend the grave it became neglected and left to the elements it became overgrown and covered with grass and moss. Anne's followers complained that they could not locate her grave and when they did were shocked to see it neglected. They acted, cleaned the stone and painted the lettering black. Local people were not too happy about this, stating that at night the headstone was too macabre compared to its darker companions.

In 1960, the then Vicar of Scarborough suggested that Anne's grave is moved nearer to the parish church stressing that it was not unusual to re-intern bodies. Scarborough Corporation refused, instead deciding to spruce the area up giving Anne a garden surrounding her grave. After the planting came a ceremony and people flocked from far and wide to witness prayers over the respected author's grave presided over by the Queen's Chaplain Canon GWO Addleshaw.

In 2013 to ensure that future visitors would be able to read the inscription on Anne's grave for years to come, the Bronte Society installed a plaque alongside the original one.

People continue to pay their respects to Anne Bronte who is remembered as one of the first literary genii who paved the way for female writers worldwide.

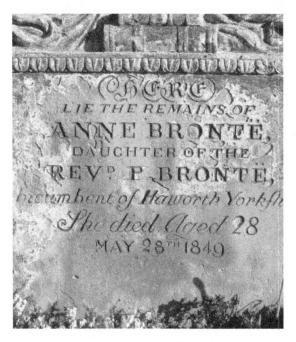

*

Scarborough a Changing Town

By the beginning of the Victorian era, Scarborough was changing rapidly. Newborough or New Borough as it was thought of and pronounced by many locals simply as 'Newbruff' together with Queen Street offered lodging houses for the increased number of visitors to the town. A narrow opening led to Long Room Street, where there were two public rooms for entertainment: Newstead and Donners. New buildings were also beginning to spring up on the cliffs and crowds would greet visitors to advise them on where to lodge, eat, bathe and dress.

Newborough ended on the short narrow street known as Carr Street which ran into Leading Post Street, Merchants Row, and leading to West Sandgate. A narrow approach led into St Nicholas Street (Long-Room Street). Gardens known as The Bowling Green ran almost the length of St Nicholas Street and were admired by many.

In 1791, a petition was presented to parliament by Scarborough Corporation, which speaks of a coach road named St Nicholas Road which led to the end of St Nicholas Cliff, and a place called Harding's Walk. These places were in a dilapidated state of repair. Shortly afterwards Huntriss Row, Falconers Road and Vernon Place were built.

Four windmills were belonging to flour mills in town, namely Greengate Mill, at the foot of Mill Street, North Marine Road which was formerly known as Greengate Lane. Albion Mill was on North Cliff, Common Mill, was on the corner of Mill Street and Victoria Road, and Harrison Mill which stood on South Cliff where St Martins Church stands.

*

Scarborough Corporation

ARMS OF THE BOROUGH.

A charter dated 22nd November 1356, confirmed the immemorial rights vested in the civil administration of Scarborough. Thus, 44 persons managed the town's affairs (not the Castle) and were in charge of the town's defences and the repair of the Pier, this consisted of;

2 Bailiffs

2 Coroners

4 Chamberlains

36 Common Councillors (divided into three sets of 12 known as the three twelves)

The first grant of morage (tolls) for enclosing and fortifying the town came in the reign of Henry III who granted a duty of 1/- on every vessel going in and out of the port laden with corn/fish, for smaller vessels the levy was sixpence and every other boat twopence and every cart twopence.

This arrangement continued for five centuries except for the reign of Richard III, who changed the constitution of the borough by appointing a Mayor, Sherrif, and 12 Aldermen. He also granted the amalgamation between Scardeburgh and the Manor of Whallesgrave (Falsgrave) into one entire county and utterly separate from the town of York. After the death of Richard III (1485) the constitution of Scarborough returned to its original ancient mode of governing.

Scarborough also had the privilege of returning two members to represent the town in Parliament, which for the size of the town was a gross over-representation, bearing in mind that towns such as Leeds, Birmingham, and Sheffield had to make do with one representative, which suggests that there must have been some great influence at Westminster to keep the borough's medieval privilege.

For centuries, prominent businessmen, merchants, shopkeepers and their immediate families dominated the Corporation. The Thompson family had provided a bailiff to the town eighteen separate times. Furthermore, the historian Thomas Hinderwell confirmed that since 1811, fifty places were available on the corporation which was filled by only fifteen families.

When it came to election time, Scarborough was a closed shop, and the disgruntled town's inhabitants suggested that members of the Corporation sacrificed the good of the community for their personal gain, which led to discontent within the community when money intended for the improvement of the town did not go to its proposed purpose, especially the harbour.

Favouritism, bribery and corruption were widespread within the Corporation, and the Corporations finances were not open to scrutiny not even by the councillors themselves.

Aristocratic landowners dominated Parliament and argued that only people who paid taxes or owned property should be allowed to take part in politics. According to them, there was no place in politics for ordinary people especially the poor and the working class.

Before the Great Reform Act of 1832, the right to vote was not as it is today a universal right, but a privilege for the wealthiest classes of society. The right to vote depended on three things;

1. Gender. Only men over 21 could vote.
2. Property. To vote, the male must own property over a particular value, and pay taxes.
3. Location. Small rural boroughs were able to elect more MPs than much larger towns and cities.

Understandably, people were unhappy with this situation, deeming it grossly unfair, so when the Great Reform Act of 1832 had received Royal Assent, people of Scarborough rejoiced to believe that this new Act would give many more people the right to vote. So much so, that in June 1832, there were bonfires in Newborough, and another one on the foreshore sands which was kept alight with old ship timbers, and tar barrels. The following day a parade passed through the town, down to the shore with 44 effigy dolls each dressed as a member of the Corporation. The protestors dug a hole in the sands, and the 44 effigy dolls were then ceremoniously buried. This was a convincing demonstration against a municipal government which had existed for 500 years. Through the years there had been previous attempts to take control of the 44 self-elected burgesses, without success.

Discontent continued throughout Scarborough, and in November 1833, two of his Majesty's Commissioners were appointed to investigate the state of the Corporation. Named as Judge and Jury were Commissioners Dwarris and Rumball.

Facing the questioning was:

John W Woodall (Jr)

(town clerk John Woodall (bailiff)

William Thornton (bailiff)

Edward Hebden (coroner)

Henry Fowler (coroner)

Anthony Beswick

William Travis

Edward Donner (The Corporation Solicitor)

Cross-examining this committee was:

Samuel Byron – Shipowner.

John Hesp G Davies

William Page.

Prior to the Commissioners' investigations, the Corporation held a meeting, at which the following resolution passed, that 'with every sentiment of duty and affection to the King and with respectful deference's to His Majesty's Commissioners, this Corporation humbly feels that it is cumbent to record a protest against a measure which appears to them to establish an iniquitous and dangerous precedent not authorised by Parliament nor recognised by the law of the land.

However, having no unworthy motive for concealing the affairs of the Corporation, desirous of affording every information within our power. The town clerk (Woodall) is authorised in his official capacity to make such answers to the said commissioners as in his discretion as he deems fit and proper.'

Mr Woodall, then declared that for some time the corporation considered the inquiry was not compulsory, and that he had confirmed this opinion with Sir James Scarlett and other legal authorities.

However, whatever the constitutional question in this regard, the corporation had nothing to conceal, and were most willing to divulge to the public any injustice; the corporation was most willing to make such voluntary statements as they were in possession of including all records and charters that he (Woodall) and a committee of friends had prepared, which would form the basis of his evidence.

The inquiry lasted two days and following the departure of the Government Commissioners, the Corporation hastily tried to cover up the findings of the report by publishing their version of accounts which stated;

'Commissioner Dwarris commented that the Corporation met the inquiry in a credible manner, which had enhanced their public spirit.' Furthermore, according to the statement the commissioners had also said;

'We cannot congratulate the Corporation of Scarborough on the complete and satisfactory refutation on all the charges brought against them and their friends, and it will be no less mortifying for those who have made themselves so conspicuous to their accusers!'

A statement from the committee members confirmed that: 'Considerable discussion took place when the revenues of the Corporation came under scrutiny, especially about the sale of common lands. They are pleased to announce that it was proved beyond doubt that the Corporation had not alienated any of the corporate property, except to defray a debt contracted for public purposes. To which, the Government Commissioners said they had acted judiciously, and that the charge that land was sold to members at a nominal price disproved, on the contrary, the Corporation negotiated the full market price, and that any surplus revenue from this sale was spent on the benefit of the town.'

Understandably, the Commissioners were not impressed with the Corporation's attempt to manipulate the findings of the inquiry. So much so they found it necessary to issue their statement, which in comparison was pejorative and concluded that the Corporation had mismanaged the town for many years and that there was indeed a great prevalence of family influence within the Corporation. This 'family influence' concluded that at the time of the commissioner's inquiry on the Corporation there were:

5 Woodalls

5 Fowlers

3 Travis'

3 Coulson's

3 Wharton's

It revealed that outside the borough the residence of certain people to attend Town Hall meetings were grounds for disqualification. One member had lived in London for four years; one lived in Beverley, one Malton, one in Filey. One member had even emigrated to Tasmania, and the collector of customs at Whitby had been absent for 30 years. One member had only attended one meeting in 45 years.

Consequently, the report deemed that one-quarter of its members were 'unfit and improper'.

The Town Clerk (John Woodall) was using the Town Hall for his private law firm (Woodall, Donner & Woodall).

Questions were raised as to the whereabouts of many charitable donations given or bequeathed to schools, almshouses and hospitals. Furthermore, it became apparent that twelve years earlier valuable land belonging to the Corporation had been sold at a nominal price to four members of the Corporation without consultation and public notice. The report also pointed out that the Corporation continued to privatise land that it held since 1257. After the reform act of 1832, the Corporation sold twenty-one acres of prime land for the sum of, eighteen hundred and thirty-five pounds to four members of the 'Old Bank' belonging to John Woodall who was then the town bailiff.

On another occasion, in cross-examination, witness Samuel Byron asked about the whereabouts of a sum of money amounting to thirty-seven pounds during the election of 1832 and was told that 'it went to the poor'. Byron was livid at this response and angrily declared 'this is the greatest mockery of the word charity that I have ever heard!' The red-faced Corporation quickly changed their stance stating that by the word poor they had meant populace. Still not impressed Byron shouted, 'Don't you mean that this money was divided between 18 of the town's publicans at the sum of two guineas each in return for a vote to Colonel Trench (Tory) in the last Parliamentary elections.'

Colonel Trench was a hard-line tory and against reform, who had told the fishermen of Scarborough that reform was uncalled for and unnecessary. Much to the surprise of the 'True Blue' Tory Corporation Trench came last in the election with only 145 votes which were for the most due to the backing of the corporation who had supplied 'blue drink in the form of free ale to the members convincing them to back Trench. This 'blue drink' was supplied by Corporation official Edward Donner who in addition to him being a councillor also happened to be a wine merchant. Two successful pro-reform Whigs, Sir John VB Johnstone of Hackness and Sir George Cayley of Brompton, represented the town in 1832.

According to Byron, even the granting of publican's licences was shady, with permissions issued without question to members of the Corporation who also owned public houses such as Bleach House (The Crown Tavern). An accusation quickly rebuffed, because the granting of this licence was only that the premises were 'convenient and on a good road for access to the Mere'.

The commissioners also discovered that monies received from Newcastle and Sunderland through the levies on loaded carriers in total had exceeded the Corporation's expenditure on the harbour. With a degree of wit and sarcasm, the commissioner asked 'was this surplus applied to eating, drinking and other useful purposes?' bearing in mind that the Corporation had declared that the Pier was in 'A good state of repair when in reality the Island and Vincents Pier were in a disgraceful condition and nothing more than a public nuisance.'

The Corporation continued in the same form until 1835 when it came to light that the Corporation had been giving away 'blue leases' for many years to friends and relatives and people with influence. For example, part of St Nicholas Cliff had been leased at a measly 5 shillings a year for a 50-year lease to a Miss Harrison. Morrison & Chapman had been granted a seven-year lease at 10s per annum for the hiring of bathing machines, and as there was no competition, they could charge what they wanted. If the Municipal Corporations Act was not rushed through Parliament, Scarborough Corporation would have leased away the town for personal benefit.

Following, the new Act, Scarborough together with many other Corporations across the country were abolished. In its place was a resident, rate-paying male electorate of 549. However, while this new legislation gave many more people the right to vote it had virtually no effect on the working class, as the right to vote depended on if you owned property and paid certain taxes. Understandably, over the proceeding years, many calls were made for further parliamentary reforms.

As a result of this new legislation, the town retained its ancient borough boundaries, although now they were divided into North and South with nine places. The old regime was dead and buried, with only John Woodall who resided at Belvoir Terrace, the only member of the old administration to survive this devastating defeat. The nemesis of the old corporation Samuel Byron who lived at 7, Granby Place was elected the town's mayor, much to the delight of the burgesses. At long last improvements began to happen to the town.

*

The Harbour & The Pier

Photo Credit Scarborough Friends Reunited. (Facebook)

There has been a pier in Scarborough for many years, which was in a poor state of repair. The pier, for the security of the shipping, dates its origin from the time of Henry III, (1207-1272) who made a grant of 40 oaks from his woods for the construction of a harbour at Scarborough.

In the 36th year of his reign, Henry III granted to the bailiffs, burgesses, and inhabitants, specific duties to be taken on all merchants' ships and fishing vessels, 'to make a new port with timber and stone.' (source Genuki) This pier was an ancient structure and not suitable for the needs of the town. There was a lighthouse at the end of the old pier which gave a signal by day and light at night to denote the proper time for ships and boats to enter the harbour.

In 1546, not only the users of the harbour but also local property owners had to contribute to its upkeep. The people of Scarborough were not happy with this arrangement and petitioned Queen Elizabeth who granted royal aid in the form of five-hundred pounds in cash, 6 tons of iron and 100 tons of timber to aid the rebuilding of the harbour.

In the year 1732, George II passed an act for enlarging and renewing the pier and the harbour which by now was in a dangerous and dilapidated state, so much so that many ships were driven against the rocks following violent storms, the pier and harbour offering no shelter.

The cost to renew the pier was twelve-thousand pounds. William Lelam along with other engineers was employed to extend the pier from near the old locker-house westward and curving it out to sea at the extremity. Engineer William Vincent took over as the engineer, and the project was completed in 1746. According to Hinderwell 'The whole of this pier is still to be known as 'The Old Pier,' but the new section should thereafter be known as 'Vincent's Pier' after the engineer who finished it.' (The new part was at the time of building easily distinguishable near the locker-room and recognisable from the different modes of building and the greater regularity of the stones.) (Hinderwell)

Tragedies were commonplace at sea, and understandably there were many superstitions among the fishermen and their wives. One was that you could not sail in a new boat on a Friday, and neither was a ship allowed to sail from the yards on a Friday. Another superstition was that it was unlucky to speak to each other when going out to sea, so silence it was otherwise the voyage would be an unfortunate one. Another curious custom amongst wives and sweethearts was to go to Vincent's Pier to appease the angry waves to obtain a promising breeze to ensure a safe return for the fishermen. About forty paces along the pier was a circular hole among the stones where women would pour into it a tepid solution of saline libation to Neptune; ancient heathen mythology designed to keep the men safe when out at sea. Terrible storms and violent seas were commonplace, and the women went through many anxious times, it is understandable that they clung to such strange superstitions.

The new pier was over 1300 feet in length and built with stones from the nearby White Nabb Quarry transported in flat-bottom boats known as 'floats' and placed at their destination by a simple mechanical invention constructed for the purpose. This quarry was a natural source of local interest and situated about a mile from Scarborough 'Spaw'. It contained large masses of stones and flat rocks some weighing 20-30 tons.

This new structure took 26 years to complete. A lighthouse was also added to this extension but was demolished in 1914 following the German bombardment, though rebuilt in 1936.

The West Pier was completed in 1822 by Engineer William Chapman and extended many times to eventually incorporate Outer Island Pier. In 1928 Corporation Wharf (North Pier) was constructed and another extension called Chicken Walk Jetty was added making access for vessels easier.

There was a duty imposed upon all ships laden from Newcastle and other ports. With revenue from the tolls due to increased shipping, the pier extended again in 1753. Opposition to the tolls was rife, and many shipbuilders from the Tyne refused to pay claiming there were no legal powers for the enforcement of these tolls and that they were 'unjust and scandalous'. The tolls were previously collected on a voluntary basis. In 1845, Scarborough Corporation took one of the ship-owners – a man called Jonasshon – to court for the outstanding toll of 8d which the ship-owner refused to pay. After a lengthy court case a jury returned a verdict finding that the warrant had not passed the great seal, Judge Baron Rolfe, therefore, entered a general verdict to be entered for the defendant. Mr Jonasshon was triumphant and highly regarded for his public-spirited actions.

Shipbuilding & Fishing

Shipbuilding in Scarborough was once a busy and thriving industry and an important part of Scarborough's heritage. The shipyards extended along the foreshore from the pier to King Richard's house. Launching was done in cradles on an inclined plane at low tide.

One of the oldest recorded shipbuilding families was the Cockerill family with launch ways adjoining Smithy hill. John Cockerill was churchwarden in 1673. James Cockrill was a bailiff in 1688. In 1690 they lived at Paradise House.

Another prominent and well-respected shipbuilding family was the Tindall family, whose name became an integral part of Scarborough society. In 1822, the Tindall's won a lawsuit against Scarborough Corporation claiming that they were in possession of Smithy Hill situated opposite the Little Island Pier as 'Kings Tenants' since 1691 in the reign of Charles II and that they were shipbuilding in Scarborough before that date.

The first known shipbuilder (Tindall family) was William Tyndale who was a 'free common counsellor' for the town of Scarborough since 1681. The Tindall family originated from East Grimston.

The Tindall daughters married into shipbuilding families such as the Cockerill family, the Mores and the Sollit's. Soon, the families were intertwined and succeeded John Cockerill in the house, which was later 51, 51a, and 52 Sandside. Then these three properties formed one building known as Ivy House. The family also bought the old Town Hall on Sandside and turned it into a Bethel for Seamen.

Other shipbuilders in the seventeenth century were Robert Hudson, who is 1641 owned part of Sandhill and Malthouse Hill and Christopher Harrison who owned the rest of Sandhill up to 1634, succeeded by the Dodsworths, Coopers, Porretts, Allatsons, and Richard Bilborough.

In the fifteenth/sixteenth/seventeenth centuries, it was not unusual for a ship to be left in a will or even shares in a vessel left in stocks to family members. (M. Andrews 1947)

Sons of shipbuilding families went to sea at the age of 14 as an apprentice. Second mate at eighteen, first mate at nineteen and it was not unusual to be master of your ship by the age of twenty-one. By the year 1765, the remuneration for the Captain of a Tindall ship would be ninety-six pounds per annum.

In 1848, the barque 'Robert Watson' from Newcastle delivered a cargo of wood to Tindall's yard together with hundreds of cocoanuts never seen in Scarborough. Over the years nearly 42,000 tons of ships were made by Tindall's yard and 30,000 by other yards between 1742 and 1879. Some of Tindall's ships were The Alfred, Fortitude, and The Free Briton. (Scarborough Maritime Heritage.)

The Tindall yard closed in 1863, and the property was put up for sale.

EXTENSIVE SALE OF SHIPBUILDERS' PLANT, SCARBOROUGH.

TO BE SOLD BY AUCTION, BY MR. J. R. HALLIDAY,

On MONDAY. May the 25th, and following Days,

THE Entire Stock of Messrs. R. W. H., and R. H. TINDALL, Shipbuilders, Scarborough, comprising:

86 Loads of		TEAK TIMBER and PLANK.
33	,,	AMERICAN ROCK ELM TIMBER.
19	,,	WHITE IRON BARK TIMBER.
27	,,	YELLOW and RED PINE, AMERICAN OAK and PITCH PINE TIMBER.
16	,,	MAHOGANY TIMBER and PLANK.

240 Tons of ENGLISH OAK TIMBER.
Sundry PLANK and YELLOW PINE DEALS.
Several ENGLISH ELM KEELS.
23 Tons of BAR IRON.

Bolts, Nails, and Sundry Iron Work; Blacksmith's Bellows, Anvils, Tools, &c., &c.

Catalogues are now ready, and may be had on application at Messrs. Tindall's Office, Sandside, or to Mr. J. R. Halliday, Auctioneer, 13, Granby Place, Scarborough.

The Auctioneer respectfully announces that the Sale will commence each day at Ten a.m., and One p.m., excepting Mondays, when, for the convenience of parties coming from a distance, the Sale will begin at One p.m.; and he intends to offer the Wood as it stands in the Catalogue until Thursday night, and on Friday morning commence selling the Iron and Blacksmith's Tools, and continue until all is sold.

13, Granby Place, Scarborough, May 8, 1863.

*

Fishing

Fishing tithes for Scarborough were paid to the monasteries for the right to fish the seas and paid according to the type of vessel used, the species of fish caught, or area worked. In the early 14th century hundreds of ships are recorded as landing herring at Scarborough during each year's season. The English boats came from all over – the majority from Lincolnshire, East Anglia and Kent, but others came from as far away as Devon and Cornwall. Many foreign vessels also fished, Flemish and French in particular.

In the early 19th century Scarborough fishermen worked without compassion or interest in their industry, dismayed that they had no available means to transport their catch. Local historian Thomas Hinderwell made no bones about exerting his opinion of the Scarborough fishing industry saying, 'the fishermen lacked interest and initiative,' with Scarborough fishermen stating that 'fishing in Scarborough was not productive,' but Hinderwell pointed out that Filey fishermen managed to bring in a good catch in similar circumstances.

Scarborough fishermen complained that they had no means of moving fish due to transport difficulties. However, in 1830-38 this all changed as Scarborough was increasing in size and the tourist industry booming.

Quite by chance a boat belonging to the Scarborough fishing fleet fishing near the Dogger Bank got separated from the rest and had not had the opportunity to haul in her nets. When the skipper did, he was amazed to find that his nets were brimming with the sole. This area was from then on known as 'the silver pit' and was a much-needed boost to Scarborough's fishing fleet which continued until 1838.

With the opening of the railway in 1845, the fishermen did, at last, have a means of moving their catch around the country. Throughout the nation, trawling increased. For the first time, railways carried fresh fish to Britain's industrial heartland. Previously fish discarded by Scarborough boats was now sold cheaply in the cities.

There was also a boom in the inshore fisheries in Scarborough. In the 1870s Scarborough had 40 cobles compared to just 6 in the 1820s. Fresh crabs could be transported vast distances by train. The remainder could be sold along the pier front. (Scarborough Maritime Heritage)

The fish market was on the sands close to the harbour, selling fresh cod, haddock, ling, turbot, skate, sole, coalfish, crabs and lobsters.

For ten weeks during the herring season between the years of 1890-1914, a group of Stalwart Scottish girls would follow the herring fleet down the east coast. The girls would stay in local lodgings and at the end of the season would take a significant sum home to Scotland for their families. Each girl could gut 50 herrings a minute which were then packed in salt at the rate of 1000 per barrel and exported. The town must have smelled slightly pungent, but still, visitors enjoyed seeing these girls working on the piers and harbourside pickling and packing herrings.

Throughout the years, there has been much talk regarding the decline of the herring fishing industry; predictably if a species travels 6 miles long and 4 miles wide, it is likely to be fished to extinction. As technology improved during the 19th-century fish stocks became strained, and in the 20th century the industry effectively killed itself off. (Scarborough Maritime Heritage)

*

Tunny Fishing (Tuna)

Tunny fishing, a sport practised by wealthy aristocrats and military officers, was primarily a sport only carried out in the Atlantic and the Mediterranean, but with the waters around Scarborough getting warmer fishing of this large, powerful fish known to be the strongest fish in the world began on the coast.

Soon after came a club known as The British Tunny Club with its headquarters on Sandside. Big game sea angling and especially tunny fishing was a popular sport attracting many famous people such as Walter Guinness, Charles Laughton and many other glamorous people.

In early September 1929, a Yarmouth steam drifter 'The Ascendant' landed a giant tunny fish weighing almost 700lbs and 9ft 9inches long at Scarborough. Skipper Captain King, reported that he had fed the fish with herring from the side of the boat, while the engineer caught it by sticking a hook through its body then they managed to haul it over the side of the boat until they could land it in the harbour when it was pulled in with a crane onto the pier. This large tunny became a tourist attraction and visited by many people.

Mr Lorenzo Mitchell-Henry son of a wealthy financier, who had vast experience of the sport in various areas of the world and who is responsible for popularising Scarborough as a tunny fishing port, caught the first tunny with a rod/line in British waters.

The first tunny caught on rod/line in British waters caught on 27th August 1933 by L Mitchell-Henry.

*

Due to the war and technical developments in herring fishing, mackerel stocks declined, thereby leading to the demise of tunny fishing.

The tunny club on Sandside is now a well-respected and popular fish restaurant.

The North Pier

THE NEW PIER AT SCARBOROUGH.

Following, the success of seaside pleasure pier's around the country. Scarborough wanted to follow suit. A consortium of prominent men namely, Woodall, Leckenby, and Hammond from Raven Hall formed a company named 'The Scarborough Promenade and Pier Company' and registered it under the companies act of 1862 with limited liability. Shares sold on the basis that the company intended to provide the numerous visitors of the rapidly increasing watering-place of Scarborough and inhabitants of the town and neighbourhood, with a handsome and commodious promenade and a convenient landing place for steamers and pleasure boats.

Shares in the company quickly sold, and the company engaged the services of Mr Eugenius Birch from Westminster Chambers. Birch was the leading architect on the design of piers and bridges around the coasts of the United Kingdom, and he had received much praise for his design of Brighton Pier. Designs were agreed, and work commenced on the project in 1866 at the cost of over twelve thousand pounds. The contractors were JE Dowson of Victoria Street, followed by Messrs Head, Wrightson & Co of Stockton on Tees.

The pier was at the centre of North Bay close to Clarence Gardens and access to it was via a slip road adjacent to a new road constructed at the expense of the town.

Constructed of iron to the plans of Birch's design the pier was 1000 ft in length and 23ft wide the head itself over 140 ft long and 50 feet wide. A commodious saloon erected for entertainment featured top named acts. Landing inclines were available for all states of the tides including steamers, yachts, and open boats.

Entertainment consisted of daily concerts and dancing on the pier every evening.

Shareholders received dividends in the initial years, but despite the pier being a distinctive feature of Scarborough, it was not the anticipated financial success the shareholders expected.

An AGM of the shareholders was held in February 1888, stating that the company was in financial difficulty and losing money, and that money owed to the bank the sum of twelve hundred and sixty pounds. The shareholders recommended that the directors should consider selling, winding up or re-constituting the company.

In September 1904, the pier was put up for auction and bought for three-thousand five-hundred pounds by Mr William Morgan the Mayor of Scarborough and the owner of the Aquarium and The People's Palace. Unfortunately, despite the low-price Mr Morgan's luck soon ran out as the following year the pier suffered structural damage from a violent tidal wave that raged war on the coast. The storm caused havoc with areas of the town strewn with debris, roof tiles were dislodged from rooftops scattering the streets.

*

Credit Paul Thomas.

Swept away in the storm was the total length of the promenade decking between the entrance to the pier and the pavilion together with the iron girders.

Foreshore Road was scattered with debris from the pier. The Japanese café was still standing, but the windows were all blown in, and the flooring was torn up. The Pavilion was completely isolated and separated from the remnants of the pier.

The Pavilion interior. Credit Paul Thomas.

A witness to the catastrophe who was working on the construction of the new Marine Drive stated, 'I heard a loud crack, and then the whole thing collapsed like a deck of cards.' (Yorkshire Post) Ironically, when the pier was offered for sale the auctioneer stipulated that 'there were certain improvements of at least five-thousand pounds needed to prevent the constant ravages of the sea on the pier'. He also advised that 'the pier be raised six to eight feet, together with a jetty to allow pleasure steamers to leave or call for passengers.

It seems that Mr Morgan did not have enough time to implement the auctioneer's suggestions. Unfortunately, for him, the pier was not insured and was destroyed and dismantled shortly after the disaster.

*

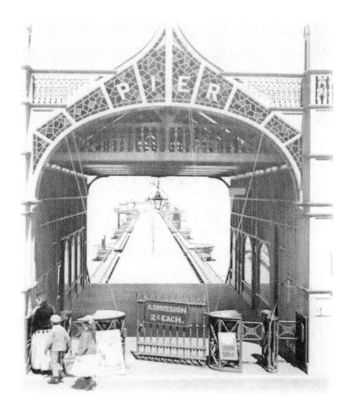

Promenade Pier Pavilion. Credit Paul Thomas.

Many acts performed on the pier during its relatively short lifespan, but for one entertainer Scarborough proved to be a fatal choice of venue. Herr Adalbert Frickell, a German conjurer, was scheduled to perform his favourite act entitled 'Novel Illusions' at the Promenade Pier Pavilion in August 1889. Before the performance, Frickell fell ill during dinner at the lodging house of Mr Thomas Rowntree of 4, Sandringham Street, Scarborough. He started to cough uncontrollably, and he ran into the backyard where he coughed up a significant amount of blood, fell to the ground and died immediately.

The police and medical officers assisted, but there was nothing that Dr Everly Taylor could do. The police officer PC George Normanton looked through the conjurer's possessions and discovered that Frickell was in severe financial difficulty. Mr Rowntree confirmed that Frickell said that he was separated from his wife and that they had a daughter who he adored.

A letter in the dead man's possession claimed that if he were to be found dead, then his death would indeed have been caused by poisoning!

Unknown to many people Frickell's permanent address was 80, Whitfield Road London, and that he had in his career performed at Crystal Palace, and many other well-known establishments. Unfortunately, he was finding it harder and harder to find work and his debts accumulated.

At the autopsy, Dr Taylor later confirmed that Herr Frickell's death occurred as the result of bleeding caused by the bursting of an aneurysm or an internal tumour and not by poison.

The coroner stated that a letter had been received from Frickell's wife saying that she was destitute and would not be able to contribute towards her husband's funeral. Therefore, Adalbert Frickell lies in an unmarked grave at Dean Road Cemetery.

Scarborough Lifeboat

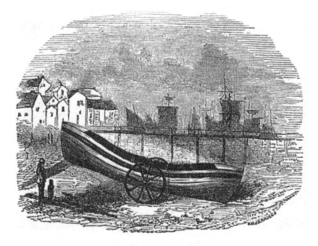

THE LIFE-BOAT.

Henry Greathead of South Shields claimed to have designed Scarborough's first lifeboat. However, Greathead's claim is disputed as both William Wouldhave and Lionel Lukin both claim to be the inventor of the first lifeboat. (Wikipedia) Nevertheless, Greathead did go on to build over thirty boats, and his designs have saved many lives over the years.

Scarborough's first boat was funded by subscriptions and donations which in 1801 had raised a total of two-hundred and twelve pounds. This first lifeboat although unnamed was known locally as 'The Greathead'. Initially, there was a boathouse at Millbeck just underneath the Spa stand. It moved in 1826, to a site near the West Pier.

Selection of the lifeboat crews came from local fishermen. Twelve men each crew, where each crew chose two steersmen and the one with the most significant boat would have the direction of the boat-crews, which should work in rotation, and would not be launched without the consent of at least one member of the lifeboat committee. The first coxswain was John Harwood a popular choice amongst the crew. A levy of a half-penny was placed on local shipping to appease the cost of running the lifeboat. (Scarborough Maritime Heritage)

The lifeboat, one of the first in the country, had its first outing in 1801 when it rescued seven people from 'The Aurora' from Newcastle which was approaching Scarborough harbour when it was driven ashore to the Southward, and the lifeboat launched as The Aurora was in imminent danger. Four of the crew were rescued immediately, while the remaining three crew members were seen clinging perilously to the rigging, Fortunately, for them, the brave lifeboat crew recovered them and took them aboard to safety.

In the first three months of its service, the first Scarborough lifeboat saved the lives of twenty men and goods and property to the value of one thousand pounds.

By 1822, 'The Greathead' was considered a little heavy and cumbersome and that a lighter boat was needed that could be launched quicker. A new lifeboat was commissioned and designed by James Peake and built by Robert Skelton of Skelton's shipyard (Skelton's Hill).

On 17th February 1836, the 'Skelton' lifeboat was launched to rescue a crew of a single-masted sloop named 'John' from Aberdeen and carrying a cargo of coal with a crew of fourteen seen in distress in the South Bay. Almost immediately a crowd of spectators gathered in anticipation of a drama at sea, or to offer help to the lifeboat. The crowd cheered as the lifeboat braved the tempestuous sea, but silence soon came as gigantic waves hit, capsizing the lifeboat. Unfortunately, the lifeboat was unable to right itself and remained upside down in the sand. When it eventually righted itself ten of the crew were helplessly washed overboard and catapulted into the raging sea. The poor men did not stand a chance as they were dragged down into the current and disappeared.

Ironically, all the crew from the 'John' were rescued using rocket lines fired from the shore, a system devised by Captain Manby by attaching lines to a rocket and launched over the wreck. Scarborough was one of the first ports to use this method of lifesaving. (Scarborough Maritime Heritage)

The crew members who lost their lives were;

Joseph Allen, Thomas Boyes, John Clayburn, Thomas Cross, John Owston Dale, James Day, Richard Marchman, Thomas Walker, Joseph Waugh and James Maw whose body was washed ashore eleven weeks after the tragedy. R.I.P brave men.

A disaster fund for the relief of the bereaved families raised the considerable sum of one-thousand four-hundred pounds Lloyds of London also donated twenty pounds to the crew's four survivors and twenty-five pounds in aid of the widows and children of the drowned men.

The Skelton Lifeboat was repaired and put back in service and remained in service until 1861, during which time she saved many more lives.

Scarborough's lifeboat became a part of the RNLI in 1861, and a new lifeboat named 'The Amelia' was launched. On her first outing on 2nd November 1861, she hit trouble when she attempted to rescue the crew of the schooner 'Coupland' which was drifting towards the Spa wall. The sea was so violent that the force of the waves dislodged massive stones. The crew of the lifeboat were no doubt terrified. Senior crew member Thomas Clayburn was washed up to the sea wall, but luckily, he managed to survive by hanging on to a lifebuoy, as did James Banks who was ejected a few minutes later and after a fearful struggle grabbed a lifebuoy. The oars of the lifeboat were deemed powerless against the powerful waves. The lifeboat crew threw ropes onto the promenade where a large crowd had gathered. She was drawn through the surf to a landing place at the southern end of the wall. It was here that the fatality occurred.

Having touched the ground, the men jumped out before the water had receded. Seeing the danger, men made a rush down the incline to assist them. In a moment of confusion, a fierce wave washed over and knocked all the lifeboat crew off their feet, they all scrambled to save their lives.

Unfortunately, two of the lifeboat crew, John Burton and Thomas Brewster lost their lives. A spectator, Lord Charles Beauclerk, was washed to the foot of a cliff. People tried their best to save him, but the poor man had no strength to catch the rope. Eventually, he did manage to grab it, and he was brought up to the music room at the Spa but was declared dead on arrival. He was 48 years old, the son of the 8th Duke of St Albans. The dead man held a commission in the 1st Royals and at the time of his death a Major in the Northumberland Light Infantry Militia.

Mr William Tindall the son of Scarborough's John Tindall a partner in the bank Woodall, Tindall Hebden & Co, a forerunner to Barclays Bank also lost his life that day. Despite a reward offered of twenty pounds for the recovery of his body, his remains were never found. William Tindall left an estate valued at thirty-thousand pounds which included the Wheatcroft Estate, which at that time was known as Wheatcroft Farm and tenanted providing an annual annuity for William's mother. The estate was sold in small parcels in 1929, providing the Wheatcroft Estate that we know today.

A Mr Isles lost his life and his only remains were his coat found floating on the waves.

The RNLI gave the sum of twenty-five pounds to the local fund for each of the two members of the crew and awarded posthumous Silver Medals to the three spectators who lost their lives. Michael Hick, Joseph Rutter and Oliver Sarony (photographer) also received silver medals for their efforts from the shore.

The Coupland & The Amelia. Photo credit Scarborough Maritime
Heritage

Unfortunately, both boats were wrecked. In November 1861, a Mrs
Cockroft generously donated a replacement boat which she christened
'Mary'. The Vicar of Scarborough blessed the boat.

*

Towards the end of October 1880, Scarborough suffered the worst
storms it had ever seen. Scarborough Mercury reported on 30th October
1880 that the sea was 'foaming and seething with terrible fury'.

A crowd of spectators soon gathered on the Spa promenade where
they saw several vessels driven towards the North Bay and were
apparently in imminent danger of being wrecked against the rocks of
Castle Hill. This boat the 'Mary' from South Shields consisted of a crew
of five and a boy on board. Scarborough lifeboat wasted no time and
went out to save them. Another boat 'The Black-Eyed Susan' a schooner
from Bideford went aground in front of the Spa wall 500 yards from
shore. Rocket apparatus was attempted, but sadly to no avail, so
Scarborough lifeboat under the charge of Coxswain Mr John Owston
went out and rescued the crew, one of whom had a broken leg.

Lifeboat rescues the crew of The Black-Eyed Susan. Photo credit
Illustrated London News 1880

During this terrible storm, the lifeboat went out five times and saved
the lives of 28 men from five different wrecks. A silver medal was
awarded to John Owston for his services.

John Owston wearing his silver medal. Photo credit Scarborough
Maritime Heritage.

In December 1954, the lifeboat was at sea for 5 hours escorting small vessels which were in difficulty during the gales. Tragically, the lifeboat was struck by a colossal wave near the pier as it tried to enter the harbour and capsized. Five of the eight crew members were thrown into the sea. The remaining three clung on to the lifeboat which righted itself. The crew managed to pull two men into the boat who were struggling in the water. However, three members of the team lost their lives. Thirty-year-old signalman Frank Bayes was thrown into the sea as the boat overturned. Sixty-three-year-old Jack Sheader was pulled from the sea but was declared dead on arrival when he reached the hospital. Assistant Coxswain Jack Cammish was also dragged from the water, but he did not regain consciousness.

The lifeboat was inspected and repaired and was soon back in service with a reconstructed crew in 11th December 1954.

After the disaster. Photo credit Illustrated London News - Saturday 25 December 1954

In 2016 Scarborough welcomed its new two-million-pound 'Shannon' class lifeboat funded by donations from the FW Plaxton Charitable Trust named in memory of Mr Frederick William Plaxton founder of Scarborough's coachbuilding firm. The boat is powered by water jets as opposed to the traditional propellers and is much faster than the boat it replaced. A new building was built to house the new boat as it was significantly bigger than the old one.

We are forever grateful to the brave men who risk their lives to save others.

*

Entertainment

The Cliff Bridge Company & Spa Bridge

See p 16.

GROVE HEAD, PLANTATION.

(Taken before the erection of the Cliff Bridge & Museum.)

In 1826 Mr Cattle of York together with twenty-five prominent businessmen met at The George Inn, York to discuss the proposal to connect the old cliff at Scarborough to the south cliff using a bridge.

The chairman Mr Cattle detailed the prospectus; 'That a lease of 99 years is granted to the Scarborough Bridge Company, of such portion of the cliff as may be necessary for making a footpath or terrace along the said cliff from the intended bridge to the Spa. There will be an annual rent of 5 shillings, and as such further terms as the committee will approve of, that the company do take ten shares each. The Bailiffs have the right to vote at general meetings and can also give orders on the Chamberlains for the payment of the instalments as they become due.' Scarborough Corporation approved these conditions on the premise that the company build a bridge and link all associated facilities with the town.

The Low Moor Iron Company of Bradford offered to complete the works on the bridge for a cost of two-thousand pounds and that the remainder of the money from shares sold would cover other expenses. Mr Outhet was appointed the engineer with an annual salary of two hundred pounds.

Importantly, the W was omitted from the Spa(W) for the first time.

On 29th November 1826, the first stone was laid by the senior bailiff. Mr EH Hebden. in the presence of a junior bailiff, Mr George Nesfield. A silver trowel was used for the occasion which was engraved with the Scarborough coat of arms. The plate fixed to the foundation stone was inscribed with the words 'For the improvement of the town of Scarborough and for the accommodation of visitors, this stone being the foundation of a new bridge to be called the Cliff Bridge.'

The men agreed to form a company to be called The Scarborough Cliff Bridge Company and to collect tolls from the public to use the bridge. The tolls from first of June 1827-31st May 1828 would be five per annum, two shillings for servants and children under sixteen. For inhabitants, three shillings per annum and for those declining tickets should pay one-penny every time they crossed the bridge. A toll system operated the bridge until it was bought by Scarborough Corporation.

In the first-year tolls brought in just over four-hundred pounds.

The selling of the grass on the Spa helped to subsidise this income.

Colls to Let:

SCARBRO' CLIFF BRIDGE
TOLLS TO LET.
TO BE LET BY TICKET,
(Or to the highest Bidder, as may be agreed upon at
the time), *on the Third of October next, at* THREE
o'Clock in the Afternoon, at the House of Mrs.
Hutchinson, (the Talbot Inn, Scarbro', for one
Year, from the 1st June, 1829, to the 31st May,
1830, (subject to Conditions to be then produced);

THE TOLLS arising from the Admission of
Persons passing along the Bridge, the Walk
the Spaw, and the Use of the Waters.

Whoever is the highest Bidder must, at the same
time, give Security, with sufficient Sureties, to be approved of by the COMMITTEE of the BRIDGE
COMPANY, for the due Payment of the Rent at
such time, and by such Instalments, as they shall
direct.

For further Information and Particulars, apply to
Mr. WARD, Secretary to the Bridge Company, Scarborough.

Scarbro', Sept. 5, 1828.

In the late 1930s, the Corporation abolished the toll and declared
that 'they got more complaints about the cost of the tolls on this bridge
than anything else in the town.' (Leeds Mercury, 1938)

*

The Opening of the Cliff Bridge 26th July 1827

London Illustrated News July 1827

At 6 am precisely guns were fired to represent the grand opening of the Cliff Bridge. Distinguished guests were invited to the Town Hall to commemorate this prestigious and memorable opening. The guests then proceeded in a procession to the newly built bridge in this order; Labourers employed in the construction of the bridge with their spades over their shoulders. Children from the Amicable Society School. A band of musicians. Ladies guarded on each side by a gentleman with white wands. Members of the Clergy. The Lord Archbishop of York supported but Scarborough town's bailiffs and the Town Clerk in their robes. Mr Cattle and other members of the committee.

The number of spectators was ten thousand, and Lady Ann Vernon and family honoured the procession as well as Sir John and Lady Johnstone and other eminent members of Scarborough's society.

The procession then proceeded along the new road and over the bridge to the platform and returned by the same route to the Town Hall where a sumptuous dinner was held at Donners Hotel to celebrate the occasion.

The bridge is 414 feet in length and 75 feet in height. The distance of the Promenade from the Bridge Spa is 350 yards. The bridge was considered by all to be an elegant and welcome addition to the area; highly ornamental, well-constructed and complimented the up and coming 'queen of watering places' perfectly.

SCARBOROUGH
CLIFF BRIDGE COMPANY.

THE Committee of the Scarborough Cliff Bridge Company are prepared to receive applications for the vacant situations of **Gate Keepers** at the North and South ends of the Bridge. Also, two temporary **Collectors** for the Summer months.

No applicants will be eligible who are above 40 years of age. Particulars as to salary and duties required, may be obtained on application to

ROBERT WARD, Secretary.

April 16th, 1858.

Henry Wyatt's Gothic Saloon

The powers that be had decided that Scarborough needed a new Spa and on Friday 27th August 1839 a public breakfast took place to reveal the opening of a new Spa saloon. Henry Wyatt's Gothic Saloon. This building was constructed from stone in a style called castellated gothic. Built from plans drawn from Henry Wyatt who was a young, forward-thinking architect of considerable merit. Visitors and patrons much admired the building erected by Mr John Barry.

For the opening, a procession of shareholders initially met at the Town Hall then at midday they proceeded across the Cliff Bridge to the saloon. Mr Thomas Weddell the town mayor together with his officers and followed by magistrates, clergy and 120 shareholders and visitors made a respectable gathering for the opening of this grand saloon. On arrival, the ladies and gentlemen sat down to a sumptuous lunch. The room was so full that there were insufficient seats available for the guests.

The window decorations were tasteful with evergreens and flowers. There was a toast to the Queen. Sir John Johnstone Bart pointed out the local beauty of the town as a splendid watering place and its benefits to health for its excellent waters.

The Spa promenade opened in 1839 overlooking the Gothic Saloon and designed by civil engineer George Knowles who had recently built a house for himself and his family on the new fashionable Crescent which he named Woodend. (Later known as Wood End)

*

Destructive Storm & the Spa

The Spa was struck by tragedy in February 1836 when a destructive storm destroyed many buildings on the coast including the Spa saloon.

People had gathered on the cliffs and the south sands in anticipation of a drama at sea or to help with a rescue should there be one. They weren't disappointed as soon the 'Skelton' lifeboat was called out with a volunteer crew to rescue a crew of three from the sloop 'John' from Aberdeen which was carrying cargo.

Just as the lifeboat reached the sloop, a powerful wave crashed against the lifeboat and capsized it with the crew trapped underneath. The lifeboat was firmly stuck in the sand and did not move until a wave eventually dislodged it flinging ten of the helpless lifeboat crew far out to sea. Three of the men had tied themselves to the lifeboat's armlines, which saved them from being catapulted to the dangerous tide. Another man William Mollon was flung shoreside of the lifeboat and clung there praying for salvation. On the shore the people watched in shock, then formed a human chain, linking hands hoping to protect what they thought was the lifeboat's only survivor. He was rescued and told his rescuers that three of his colleagues were in the overturned lifeboat. Fortunately, they were all rescued as were all the crew from the sloop which was saved by a rocket line.

The bodies of the eight-lifeboat crew were found the following day. Richard Marchman's body not discovered until the following May, and the body of Thomas Boyes was never recovered.

*

The wooden section of the Spa saloon was severely damaged and didn't stand a chance against the raging storm and destroyed. The section built from the stone was the only part that remained. Fortunately, the spaw wells were not buried and so would be able to function again in time. The pier and houses on Scarborough seafront were so severely damaged by the sheer violence of the horrendous storm that doors were burst with the force of the water and flung people's possessions far out to sea.

New Spa Saloon 1858

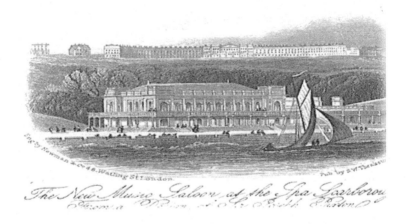

The New Music Saloon at the Spa Scarborou

Photo Credit S.W Theakston

Scarborough Cliff Bridge Company provided an additional attraction for visitors by erecting a handsome music saloon. This saloon designed by Sir Joseph Paxton and Mr GH Stokes opened to the public on 20th September 1858.

To complement this prestigious saloon the company constructed an extensive promenade which extended nearly a quarter of a mile in length giving access to visitors to the Spa. This promenade extended around the south end of the spa and faced the sea. The construction was very grand with decorative brackets and cast-iron columns. The new saloon was extremely popular and became the most successful music venue outside London.

The Spa Devastating Fire September 1876

Photo credit Scarborough Museums Trust

On the 8th September 1876, a large and fashionable crowd had attended the Spa and had enjoyed the sounds of Heir Lutz's band, at around ten in the evening the audience had dispersed. Also, to the ordinary attractions at the Spa, a grand bazaar was being held in aid of the funds of St Mary's and Christchurch churches organised by the Venerable Archdeacon Blunt. Shortly after ten o'clock, Mrs Sitwell's maid was leaving the hall noticed sparks beginning to fall from the roof and raised the alarm.

Crowds of people were seen hurrying to the scene which was quite a spectacle as the sea, the cliffs, and surrounding landscape was lit up with a lurid glow, and white showers of sparks fell onto the sands and the promenade.

It was evident that the entire block of buildings surrounding the saloon and the spacious reception rooms were doomed.

The flames shot up high into the air, and very soon the beautifully decorated vaulted roof dedicated to the arts began to fall in.

The firemen under Superintendent Pattison worked gallantly and brought in the hose and reels, but they were helpless against the raging flames, and all their brave efforts were in vain. In all the excitement there was no time to save any of the valuable property. Portions of the bazaar goods were removed and works of art rescued among them was a scriptural painting by Noel Paton aptly inscribed 'The Man of Sorrows' valued at six thousand pounds.

The source of the fire was said to have been caused by the concentrated heat in the gas 'sunlights' suspended from the roof. The Cliff Bridge Company had ensured that the building was well insured. However, Mr White who leased the refreshment rooms was not so fortunate as most of his stock was liquor which was not insured.

*

The New Spa 'Grand Hall'

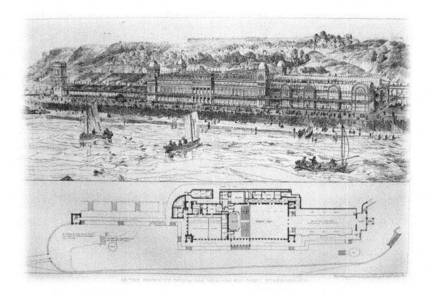

Photo Credit Colin Whitehead.

The following year, work commenced rebuilding the Spa which, after a lot of careful planning and hard work, was reopened to the public in June 1879 and considered to be one of the most elegant halls in the country.

The Old 'Gothic' Spa was rebuilt as the building was unsafe and had to be demolished. The most important part of the re-building was to ensure that the cliff behind the building was safe and twenty-five thousand tons of earth secured that the foundations were built on solid rock.

The new name for the hall was the 'Grand Hall' which accommodated one thousand people. Also, there was a low ornamental iron balustrade which provided an arena capable of holding an additional five hundred people together with standing room. The orchestra held three hundred vocal and instrumental performers. Underneath the orchestra, were dressing rooms and green rooms for performers.

The decorations were in the Italian Renaissance style in grey and gold with the walls adorned with murals in a coral-red decorative varicoloured design in what was known as canvas-plaster.

In addition to this Grand Hall, there were also rooms for a manager, a reading room, a billiard room, conservatory, café/buffet and a series of promenades at different levels, which offered a variety of great attractions to visitors who travelled to the Grand Hall from all over the country.

Author's own collection

The builders also ensured that the new building was fireproof. Throughout the years the Grand Hall has retained its elegance and continues to be a favourite place for various events from weddings to orchestras.

The company had many trials and tribulations, with storms and flooding, but they were determined to succeed.

In 1837, the manager Mr Hastings first advertised for a band of no less than eight musicians who would play every evening except Saturdays and Sundays. The cost to the company was ten pounds for the season. By 1843, this figure had risen to fifty pounds. In 1846, Mr William Watson of the Princes Theatre London was persuaded to supply a band to Scarborough for a month at the cost of eighty pounds.

By 1850, the cost of a band for the season had risen to two- hundred pounds. Two years later strings and reeds were introduced in place of some of the brass instruments, and by 1865 the cost of the 'orchestra' had risen for the first time to one-thousand pounds.

Between the years 1867 and 1879 Heir Meyer Lutz conducted an orchestra of twenty and returned between the years of 1884-1892 and was paid sixteen guineas a week, by 1894 the orchestra's cost was two-thousand pounds for the season.

In 1905, the number of musicians employed for the season had increased to thirty, when composer/conductor Alick Maclean took over and remained there for almost twenty-five years, unfortunately, Mr Maclean died on the eve of his silver jubilee anniversary.

Mr Kneale Kelly took over the orchestra for the season in 1938.

Digital Public Library of America

*

Max Jaffa

The Max Jaffa trio closed the 1958 season at the Spa, but two years later the renowned violinist and bandleader began his long association with Scarborough. Originally from London, Max Jaffa (Original name Jaff) was born in 1911 in London, the son of Israel Jaff(e), an immigrant from Latvia on the Baltic coast and his London- born Russian wife, Millie Makoff. A true southerner, Max thought that Yorkshire was all 'flat caps and hills', but soon fell in love with the beauty of Scarborough and its countryside. For twenty-seven years along with his orchestra, Jaffa entertained the locals and holidaymakers. He only missed one performance, and that was to attend his friend's funeral.

Max Jaffa died peacefully in 1991 aged eighty. To this day his music remains in the lives of many.

*

Rotunda Museum

SCARBOROUGH MUSEUM AND CLIFF BRIDGE. *1828*

The Rotunda Museum was constructed in 1828 for the promotion of science and local natural history and built to the specifications detailed by Mr William Smith, 'the father of English geology'.

William Smith was born in Oxfordshire, the son of a blacksmith. Smith published the first geological map of Britain which he based on his observation that rock layers (strata) were identified by the fossils they contain. Smith's plan and ideas were crucial in paving the way for a better understanding of geology worldwide.

Smith had various geology projects which he funded by securing a mortgage on his home. Regrettably, he soon ran into difficulties, which he tried to rectify by borrowing money from sympathetic creditors. Unfortunately, it was too late, and Smith soon found himself with serious financial problems. Smith had no choice but to sell his valuable and extensive fossil collection to the British Museum for seven hundred pounds. However, again this action was still not enough to save him, and in 1819 he lost everything and was sent to Kings Bench debtors' prison in London.

Released from prison in 1824 Smith moved to Scarborough where his talents were recognised, and he was appointed for the planning and overseeing of a new museum. Initially, the location of the museum could not be decided, with some subscribers wanting it at the end of the terrace, some preferring it to be across the road near the bridge, while others preferred Huntriss Row.

After deliberation, a suitable place was agreed, and the foundation stone laid in April 1828, by the President of the society Sir John VB Johnstone Bart in the presence of bailiff Woodall and overseen by all the members, of the Philosophical Society. The brass inscription stone has the following inscription;

This building erected for a museum by subscription of the members of the Scarborough Philosophical Society began April the 9th 1828.

The principal projectors were;

Sir JVB Johnstone, Bart, President.

Thomas Duesberry, Esq (who provided the collection of the late Mr Thomas Hinderwell Esq)

Robert Tindall, Jun Esq, Chairman of the building committee.

John Dun Esq, secretary. William Smith geologist.

Mr Bean & Mr Williamson, naturalists.

The museum was designed by Mr R K H Sharpe of York and built in the style of a rotunda of the Roman Doric. On opening, the principal room was thirty-five feet high and lit by a dome. The initial proposal was that once funds were raised then additional wings would be added. The museum opened to the public in 1828.

Unfortunately, the museum also attracted unscrupulous members of Victorian society. The local press reported that in the early hours of Sunday evening/Monday morning on 23rd July 1859 the museum was subjected to a sophisticated robbery when thieves escaped with a collection of valuable gold and precious stones, together with other treasured articles including Indian weapons set in gold. One of the weapons was shaped like a couteau de chasse. The stolen coins included British coins from the time of Canute, Harold II, Henry II and Henry III. A penny from the time of Edward the Black Prince, a gold Angel from the time of Richard III. One and five gold pieces, and some silver from Valparaiso. The shocked museum members were shocked to see that the gold had been roughly torn away from one of the scabbards of the swords, with only the centre-left behind.

The Rotunda Museum was built to Smiths design and displayed fossils illustrating his ideas. He arranged the fossils and rocks in the order which they occurred with the youngest cases at the top and the oldest at the bottom. The order around the walls reflected the order of rocks on the Yorkshire coast. A selection of the rocks on the coast was drawn around the inside of the building by Smith's nephew another geologist, John Phillips. In 1861, considerable additions were augmented to the building and wings were added to each side at a cost of six hundred pounds.

In 1920, a chest was discovered once belonging to the first Earl of Londesborough who was renowned for taking a great interest in archaeology. The chest had been left unopened since 1851 and presented to the Earl from Mr W Dossey who found the items on a barrow on his farm Warter Wold, which was near Warter Priory (demolished 1972). The chest contained five skulls, a leg, arm, and bones together with an ornate urn and a Roman vase. All these items were donated to the museum.

Scarborough Corporation took over the running of the museum in 1935 from the Philosophical Society, on the requirement that the museum would be free to the public. The society offered two hundred pounds towards the initial expense of running the museum. The building was upgraded in 2008 with the aid of a Heritage Lottery Grant and lovingly restored and updated to include a lift for disabled visitors. Rotunda is now one of the oldest surviving purpose-built museums in the country housing one of the foremost collections of Jurassic geology on the Yorkshire Coast. It is a must place to visit when in Scarborough.

*

Scarborough Britain's First Holiday Resort

Scarborough Tramway

Nine acres of land was secured on the North Bay near to the new Promenade Pier, to be converted into pleasure grounds. A small interval separated the two bays, but the ground in-between was steep and often inaccessible. The proposal was to construct on the level a well-lit ventilated tunnel which enabled a tramway to run from bay to bay. In less than 4 minutes visitors could sit in a comfortable carriage and pass from the south of the town to the north.

The surrounding grounds were laid out in an attractive form. The tramway opened to the public in October 1881. Initially, 10,000 pounds was raised in shares, which was then (and now) a considerable amount of money.

The Aquarium/Galaland

The Graphic London

A marine aquarium for living sea-animals was displayed in a large hall, glass covered with exotic ferns and plants. There was also archery, croquet, a pleasure garden and music.

Here is a copy of the share application.

FORM OF APPLICATION.
(To be retained by the Bankers.)
To the Directors of the Scarborough Sub-Tramway
Aquarium and Improvement Company, Limited.
Gentlemen,—Having paid to your credit, at the Bank,
the sum of ——— pounds, being £1 per share on ———
shares of the Scarborough Sub-Tramway Aquarium and
Improvement Company, Limited, I request you to allot
me that number of shares ; and I hereby agree to accept
the same, or any smaller number that may be allotted to
me, and to pay the balance due thereon, according to the
terms of the prospectus.
Name in full.............................
Address.............................
Profession (if any) ....
Date.....................1871.
Signature ....
(Addition to be filled up if the applicant wishes to pay up
in full on allotment.)
I desire to avail myself of the privilege to pay up in full
on allotment the above shares, in terms of prospectus.

The land was cleared to make way for the building, which was built underground on the site of an old horse and carriage site, which were demolished to make way for this new building. The architect was again the favoured Eugenius Birch who had success with an aquarium in Brighton.

The interior was spectacular, and something Scarborough had not seen before, or since. The entrance and staircase were designed in the style of a Hindu Temple. The Reading and Dining rooms resembled the Rajah Bhauldwin Singh's palace at Govardhan. The whole building has a distinctive Indian feel. Even the massive stone columns that support the roof, which is in the form of the 'Octagonal Grotto', are like the 'Caves of Elephants' in Mumbai.

There were 25 tanks of water installed for the fish; the largest tank holding 62 gallons of water. The aeration of water was due to air being forced directly into the water, thus keeping down the temperature of the water thoroughly oxygenating it.

The structure of the building itself was again uniquely built of colourful bricks of terracotta and stone. The building opened to the public on Whitsuntide Monday 1877.

The Aquarium was not without its troubles. One year after opening the management brought a court case against their ex-manager for breach of contract, and in September 1879 one of the keepers while cleaning out a tank was seized by an Octopus which grabbed him by the leg (fortunately, he had boots on). The octopus was one of the largest, and it fastened four of its tentacles around the leg of his boot, and the other four held firmly against the rocks at the back of the tank. A struggle took place, and the keeper found it difficult to disengage himself without killing the animal. Finally, he slid himself out of the boot leaving the animal clinging on and squeezing tight for a further twenty minutes.

The company struggled on but was not without its problems. Drainage was significantly problematic, especially following heavy rainfall when raw sewage and thick mud would seep through a door to the seawall which was underneath the Aquarium. The company considered suing Scarborough Corporation for loss of earnings.

The company also wanted Scarborough Corporation to reduce the ground rent on the building from five-hundred pounds a year to two-hundred. The Corporation refused. The company could no longer afford to trade, and all live animals and fish including a live alligator, seal and octopus sold.

Financial struggles continued and in May 1886 solicitors were instructed on behalf of the mortgage company under the power of sale and to offer the Aquarium for sale by public auction. The condition of the sale was that it be sold as one lot. Unfortunately, at the end of the auction, only one bid was received by a Mr Peacock who was acting on behalf of a consortium. The mortgage company rejected the proposal but agreed to speak to the consortium privately.

Following negotiations, the Aquarium sold to a syndicate of seven gentlemen from around the country including Mr William Morgan. The consortium made a statement to the press saying, 'in future, the entertainment will be arranged more for the amusement of the millions, and less for the entertainment of the select.' The company was then to be known as The Scarborough Aquarium and Peoples Palace.

The company added a zoo with exotic animals including tigers, monkeys and elephants. In 1889, one of the elephants took a dislike to a man in the audience named Mr Philburn who was a detective from Leeds and a visitor to the Aquarium. Mr Philburn had an uncanny resemblance to the animal's former keeper. This elephant did not get on well with his ex-keeper and took an instant dislike to the unsuspecting detective and gave a loud bellowing roar and knocked the man to the ground. Mr Philburn was taken to the Leeds Hotel where his injuries were deemed serious.

The onset of the war hurt visitors to the town. At an annual general meeting, it was decided to wind up the company voluntarily. The Aquarium closed its doors in 1914.

Captain Webb, the famous swimmer who was the first man to swim the channel with no artificial aids, and the man with his name and face on matchboxes, attempted a record in the Aquarium. His challenge was that he swam continually for 74 hours (he did break every so often). A large 40ft tank was provided, and Captain Webb completed his task without showing the slightest bit of fatigue, breaking another world record. Captain Webb lost his life while attempting to swim across Victoria Falls in 1883.

*

Gala Land

After the war, Scarborough Corporation bought the Aquarium and between the years 1925-1966 and thereafter it was known as Gala Land. The fish tanks were converted into shops; there were clowns, comics, jugglers, a monkey house and an alligator pond. A swimming pool was also added.

Not long after the Corporation took over, there was a terrible accident. A tram driven by 34-year-old driver Mr George Darley Smith lost control and ran backwards down Vernon Place and crashed through the glass roof of the Aquarium (Gala Land) Ballroom. Witnesses later testified at an inquiry into the incident that they saw a driver ask Mr Smith a question, but Mr Smith did not neglect his duties, they said they saw him panicking and trying desperately to apply his brakes. One of the witnesses confirmed that the train had stayed on the wire within a pole's length of the derailment and that the tram was travelling no more than 20 miles per hour.

The tram was twenty years old but had new controls fitted five years previously. Over the season before the accident, it had covered six thousand miles.

The conductor of the tram Mr Henry Wyke stated that he had only worked for the Tram company for five weeks but received training that in the case of a 'run back' his duty was to the safety of the passengers. He explained that on the day of the accident he was standing on the back platform and let the car go back five or six inches. The passengers on board began to jump off one by one. He did not make any attempt to operate the wheel or track brakes as he was under the impression that they would not work at both sides simultaneously.

As the tram crashed through the glass of the Aquarium the driver Mr Smith was not expected to be found without extreme injuries, but miraculously he was found pinned beneath the driver's seat, he had cuts to the back of his head and his forehead. He calmly smoked a cigarette while he waited for the ambulance to arrive. He was released from the hospital a few days later. Two visitors were injured in the incident, luckily both recovered.

Interestingly, one of the rescuers, a Mr Herbert Shaw who was the manager of Scarborough Corporation baths, told the press at the time that this was the second time that he had rescued Mr Smith. He explained that he had been at school with him and when they were schoolboys, they both played near Wilson's Wood with a 'bogey', which they used to carry clay down to the lower end of the dell. One time the bogey got out of control, and all the boys on her jumped clear. All the boys except for Smith who landed on a pond at the bottom of a steep incline. Shaw said that he had to pull Smith out of the pond with a pole.

Gala Land continued but was not a significant success. In 1938 the corporation consulted engineers and Professor SD Adshead in his role as a town planning consultant, who suggested that, along with other improvements to the town, the Corporation demolish Gala Land and replace it with an underground car park, while above this should be an attractive garden with ornamental pools. The war followed, and the plans shelved. In 1966, Gala Land closed its doors for the last time. The building was demolished and is now the underground car park that we see today.

*

Transport & the Railway

Before the opening of the railway, transport to and from Scarborough was a long and uncomfortable journey. The roads were not good, as the Yorkshire Gazette reported in 1821, 'The road between Scarborough and York is in a bad state of repair, and it is a heap of un-fashioned materials collected together in great quality which are thrown together without method or plan. The public is permitted to scramble as best they can.'

Subsequently, a new road was needed, and in 1821 surveyors McAdam & Son were appointed to renew this road. This new road would eventually save a considerable amount on each of the various parishes who were at that time spending substantial amounts of money in constant repairs to this road.

Scarborough had a couple of carriages that left Scarborough to York two days a week. There was Thomas Burniston who lived near the gates, and Sarah Craggs who lived at the bottom of Newborough, both left Scarborough for York at midday on Mondays and Thursdays. Mr Porter Owston set off for Bridlington from the Star Inn King Street at nine Tuesdays and Fridays and returned at six in the evening Mondays and Thursdays.

Horses were also let out, Mark Dove and William Peacock from Queen Street, and Matthew Beecroft from without the gates. William Donkin (Blind Billy Donkin), a poor blind man from Halls square, has an elegant pony carriage which he let out at a reasonable rate.

The road from Scarborough and York was not without problems, and highway robbery happened quite frequently. On one occasion a Mr

Joseph Webb who was the innkeeper at The Bell Inn, Scarborough was returning from Bridlington in a gig when three men approached him. One man took hold of the horse's rein then whistled for the other two men who came running from their hiding place. Mr Webb quickly realised what was happening and took hold of the whip and set off at full gallop. He wasn't quick enough as one of the robbers pointed a gun at Mr Webb's head and yelled 'Give me all your money or I will blow your brains out!' Bravely, he whipped the horse, and the horse sped off. When Mr Webb looked behind him, he saw all three men standing on the road. He realised how lucky he was, as if the robber had fired the gun, he would have lost his life. Mr Webb had seen the men as it was a moonlit night and he said that the gunman wore a blue-green coat. The perpetrators were never found.

On another occasion, a coachman took pity on an old lady and her son who were travelling between York and Scarborough and compassionately offered them a lift. Soon after, the woman and her son cut open several boxes, stealing trinkets and parcels, and escaped with the goods. The couple was apprehended in a small lodging house in Malton, and the stolen articles were found in their possession.

*

The Railway

Author's own collection

In 1840, Mr George Hudson is known as 'The Railway King' and chairman of the York and North Midland Railway attended a meeting at Scarborough Town Hall to listen to views on the possibility of opening a railway line in Scarborough. The meeting mutually decided the benefits that this line would bring to the town especially with regards the profitability that the increased number of visitors, who would be able to travel more freely from all corners of the country, would bring.

Mr Hudson stipulated that the Scarborough line would be one of the cheapest lines to construct in the country. Therefore, Hudson appointed engineer Robert Stephenson to oversee the project. Objections to the plans were minimal, with most people agreeing that, with the addition of a railway to Scarborough, it would become the foremost East Coast resort. Royal assent received, and the 43-mile line was completed in just over one year, mainly due to the planners deciding to build the route around the River Derwent which is a slower route but is a more scenic approach.

The official opening took place on Monday 7th July 1845, when thirty-five carriages each carrying 18 people and headed by locos Hudson and Lion left York bound for Scarborough around 1.30 pm. Along the route crowds of spectators gathered, on the riverbank people cheered and waved their hats, handkerchiefs and their parasols. The train stopped briefly at Castle Howard where passengers enjoyed ale and refreshments.

When the train arrived in Scarborough, the station was packed to the rafters. The town had declared a day's holiday and all shops were closed to mark the event. An elegant lunch was laid on for the dignitaries. George Hudson gave a toast to 'the health of Scarborough Corporation'. The company then formed a procession and to a band of music they paraded through the town.

The party returned to York where the festivities continued. Viscount Morpeth (Castle Howard) gave a statement poetically stating: 'Railways develop and diffuse the resources of the national wealth. Railways are the means of bringing whatever product it may be, the oaks that stud the meadow, the larches that range from the uplands to the workshop of the mechanic, or the wharf of the shipbuilder. Railroads not only carry comforts to the rich man's door, but they also light the fire in the poor man's hearth.' (Hull Packet, July 1845)

Mr George Townsend Andrews designed the original station building, which included a 348-foot-long wrought iron roof, which was fully glazed. It stood 30 feet over the tracks. Its span was 88 feet, and it was a superb sight. The station consisted of two platforms (more were added later) a large central booking office, a superintendent's room, a second-class waiting room, toilets, porters' room, first-class waiting room, ladies waiting room, and a refreshment room. Above this room was a ten-bedroom hotel which was previously intended to be the stationmaster's house. Potts of Leeds designed the station clock at the cost of one hundred and ten pounds. Lighting at the station was by gas and Scarborough Corporation undertook the maintenance of the building.

*

Part Three Buildings, Hotels, and People

As travel became more accessible the population of Scarborough gradually increased. Prominent houses were built to accommodate the fashionable clientele who were moving into the area. John Uppelby, a local solicitor and town clerk who had business premises on Sidney Place, went into partnership with builders John & William Barry and in 1825 they acquired land from the wealthy banker and shipowner, John Tindall with the intention of building a crescent of elegant houses.

Architects, Richard Hey Sharp and Samuel Sharp of York were commissioned to design the project, which was to build a crescent together with seven prominent houses overlooking the cliff. The building initially went as planned, and soon The Crescent and Belvoir Crescent were constructed. However, in the beginning, only four prominent houses were built (a fifth came later).

First, to be built in 1833 was Wood End completed in 1835 (later owned by the Sitwell family), followed two years later by Warwick Villa (renamed Londesborough Lodge after Lord Londesborough who bought the house in 1850). Then came East Villa which was later known as Belvoir House and then the White House, followed by Grove Villa. These houses brought an element of style and elegance to the area. A fifth house Broxholme Villa was the last to be built in between Wood End and Warwick Villa. (Londesborough Lodge)

Wood End

The first occupier of Wood End was George Knowles Esq, a retired successful civil engineer formerly of Lucan House, Sharrow, Harrogate.

Knowles had worked around the country and engaged in many public works. He was also the inventor of the new illuminating gas stove.

Mr Knowles was vehemently against the railway coming to Scarborough and wrote letters to the press denouncing it. He even at his own expense wrote and distributed a pamphlet saying, 'Scarborough is a small town except in the bathing season. One coach does all the work for eight months of the year. I fail to see what advantage a railroad would bring to the town. The inhabitants of this town are pleased to see respectable people come amongst them, they come to breathe pure air and take the waters, but they have no time or use for a great influx of vagrants and those who have no money to spend.'

Mr Knowles died on 23rd June 1866 aged 80. He is buried in the churchyard of St John the Evangelist church in Sharrow, Harrogate, a church he designed and to which he bequeathed five-hundred pounds to build a parochial school to be attached to this church. In 1867, the entire contents of Wood End were offered for sale by agents Tasker Hart. The contents included magnificent and costly furnishings, highly valuable works of art by Watteau, Snydes, Carmichael and many more, a cellar of fine wines, and various pieces of Rosewood and Mahogany furniture.

Wood End was offered for sale by auction in 1869, solicitors Woodall & Donner advertising a substantial marine residence with a 3-storey summer house, stables, coach house, pleasure-grounds and the new owner was Mr JR Halliday. Mr Halliday only stayed at Wood End for a year, and the house sold again in 1870.

Broxholme Villa

Scarborough Art Gallery Blue Plaque.

The last of the houses to be built was Crescent Villa completed in 1845. Built for solicitor John Uppelby and his family. John passed away in 1856, and his wife continued to live there until her death in 1881. The villa was then occupied by Edward Chivers Bower, the father of sculptor Lady Ethel Alice Chivers Harris, and the great-grandfather of Katherine, Duchess of Kent. Bower renamed the house 'Broxholme' after his family seat near Doncaster. The house stayed in the Bower family until 1904, then sold to Miss Mary Evelyn Maud Crompton Stansfield, whose family claimed ancestral connections to the diarist John Evelyn. Miss Stansfield used the house as a summer residence and let it out for the rest of the year.

In 1924 the house was sold to its last private owner, Henry Edward Donner, a solicitor and a member of one of Scarborough's oldest families, who renamed it 'Crescent House'. A keen gardener, Donner made many improvements to the gardens including installing the stone gateway to the old Falsgrave Strawberry Gardens, which we still see today. (Content from Wikipedia/Scarborough Art gallery)

Londesborough Lodge

The fateful visit of Prince of Wales Prince Edward 'Bertie' to Scarborough. (1871)

Lord Londesborough

William Henry Forester Denison, 1st Earl of Londesborough, known as 'Lord Londesborough' from 1860 to 1887, was a British peer and Liberal politician and a friend of His Royal Highness Prince Edward 'Bertie' the Prince of Wales. The Londesborough residence (when in Scarborough) was Londesborough Lodge, together with

Londesborough Estate where he often invited several of his wealthy and influential friends to join him for a shooting party.

Lord Londesborough was accepted as part of the 'Marlborough House Set' a group of wealthy individuals, who much to his mother's annoyance was founded by HRH Prince Edward, who on his marriage to Princess Alexandra of Denmark in 1863, was given the leases on both Sandringham and Marlborough House, together with an income of one hundred thousand pounds per year.

Edward, who had a reputation as a philanderer was only too pleased to be away from his mother's strict rule and was anxious to live the high life, and amassed friends who, like him, loved shooting, society balls, fine dining and racing. Prince Edward as the future King of England, Scotland and Ireland and the Emperor of India, saw himself above everyone else, and to be invited into his exclusive circle, the criteria was that you had to be wealthy, glamorous, sporty well- mannered and fundamentally amusing!

Lord Londesborough, who at the time was reputed to be one of the wealthiest peers in England, loved the arts, and any sport so he was a perfect candidate to be accepted into the Prince's clique. The Lord was a patron of the stage, who was reported to have lost thirty thousand pounds in one production named 'Babel & Bijou' deemed 'a musical spectacular', but it was quite the opposite, and the production was an immediate flop.

Sitwell describes the Lord as 'A person of extreme elegance & splendour, he shines wherever he is.' Known to be dashing and stylish he was always impeccably turned out, his hair was brushed to perfection, his hat strategically in place, a pearl pin in just the right place, and just the right amount of the white of his cuffs showing always. Reports suggest that when in Scarborough Lord Londesborough would visit the beach from Londesborough Lodge on three-quarters of a mile of a red carpet. Fitting, he believed in his status. Still, being one of the 'in-crowds' came at a cost and to keep up appearances Lord Londesborough had to sell substantial parts of his estate.

Prince Albert Prince of Wales. 'Bertie'

The Prince of Wales and some of the 'Marlborough House set' had been invited to join Lord Londesborough in Scarborough on three separate occasions, in 1869, 70, and 71. The year 1871, was the most memorable but would have a devastating effect on the Prince, his friends, Lord Londesborough and the town of Scarborough itself.

Monday 4th November 1871, the Prince arrived in Scarborough accompanied by his wife Princess Alexandra of Denmark. The Royal couple and their guests met a reception at Scarborough train station and an eagerly awaited public reception. No expense was spared, and the town illuminated with bonfires and fireworks on the hilltops. There was a public reception which had been funded for months before the royal visit via subscriptions. On leaving the station the prince and his entourage were met with a 21-gun salute together with a rocket display from the nearby hills.

Amongst the guests were further members of the Marlborough House set including The Marquis of Hartington, Mr Christopher Sykes (M.P) Mr John Loraine Baldwin, Colonel Ellis, (in waiting) and the Hon Mrs Stoner (in waiting) and the 7th Earl of Chesterfield Lord Philip Arthur Stanhope MP for South Nottingham. (1860-66)

A joyful cheering crowd continued to welcome the party with the 6th North Yorkshire volunteers forming a guard of honour to Lord Londesborough's villa. The party travelled down Westborough, passing under a triumphal arch under the Bar, which was both illuminated, then down Newborough, St Nicholas Street, Harcourt Place, The Crescent. Onwards, to the Castle, South Bay and all the cliffs, which were also floodlit.

The Royal party were entertained at the Spa to a drama company who had played before to the Royal visitors.

Throughout their stay, the Lord and Lady Londesborough entertained the Royal couple and their distinguished guests. Many sporting pastimes were undertaken, such as shooting and hunting.

The party left Scarborough on the 11th November, and as the Prince and his guests aligned their car at the railway station, were greeted by the Volunteers Royal Artillery & Rifle Corps who formed a guard of honour. Crowds gathered for a last glimpse of the Prince before he returned to Marlborough House. All the distinguished guests returned to London except for Christopher Sykes (Conservative MP for Beverley) who went to his residence, and Mr John Lorraine Baldwin who stayed at Scarborough with Lord Londesborough.

The Mayor of Scarborough together with the town's vicar and members of the Corporation were all present to see the departure of the Prince and Princess and their guests. The Prince, after being introduced to the Mayor, expressed how pleased he was with the town of Scarborough in general, and how gratified he and his party were for such a cordial reception. The Prince of Wales and Lord Londesborough shook hands warmly, and the Prince told the Mayor that he would write to him shortly.

As the train moved out of the station, loud cheers were heard from the crowd, and a band played the National Anthem. A short time later a letter was received from the Prince to Lord Harcourt Johnstone Bart M.P which read; 'Sir, The Prince and Princess of Wales cannot leave Scarborough without asking you to express to the inhabitants of the town how gratified they have all been with the magnificent reception they have met with. The Royal Highnesses will not fail to convey to the Queen the cordial loyalty to her Majesty the Queen and the Royal family which has been granted here. I have the honour to be your obedient servant.'

Little was anyone to know that this would be the last time that the Prince was to visit Scarborough.

His Royal Highness returned to London in good health, however on Monday 13th November 1871, the Prince returned from a shooting party feeling ill, he complained of a chill, shivering, headache and depression. The following day he was far worse, and he developed a whitlow on his finger, and medical assistance was called in to care for him at Sandringham House. His illness quickly deteriorated, and Sir Edward Jenner diagnosed the Prince's symptoms as Typhoid Fever. The same disease which ten years earlier had claimed the life of his father.

One of the Prince's grooms at Sandringham Charles Blegg had died of the same disease, although it was confirmed that Mr Blegg had been in a poor state of health for some time and became seriously ill on his return from a trip to Scotland.

To make matters worse one of the Prince's guests who had accompanied him to Scarborough, the Earl of Chesterfield, Lord Philip Arthur Stanhope also fell ill with the same disease. Suspicions aroused as to the cause of the outbreak of this contagious disease, and the sanitary condition of Scarborough's Londesborough Lodge brought into question, and a full and thorough investigation ordered. Bulletins were issued three times a day on the state of the Prince of Wales.

A bulletin issued 1/12/1871:

'His Royal Highness the Prince of Wales has passed another quiet night and is progressing favourably, though the fever is not yet abated.'

A further bulletin was issued later in the day:

'The regular exacerbation of the symptoms which occurs towards evening was in excess in the early part of the night, but as of now the fever, although severe, is not less favourable.

Signed

William Jenner M.D.

William Gull M.D

John Lowe M.D.

*

Such was the seriousness of the Prince's illness that Queen Victoria was summoned from Osborne House to hold a vigil at his bedside with a distraught Princess Alexandra by his side.

The investigation took a turn for the worse when the Earl of Chesterfield died at his home Bretby Hall. Questions were beginning to be asked about what had happened to the Royal party while at Scarborough.

The Queen, who herself was not in good health visited her son mindful that he was suffering from the same disease that claimed her beloved husband, Albert.

*

Londesborough Lodge

Londesborough Lodge. (WikiCommons Licence)

Press reports were scornful, not only about Londesborough Lodge but with the town of Scarborough itself.

A commission was carried out by the Lancet (medical journal) on the sanitary condition of both Londesborough Lodge and Sandringham; this is what they found:

The Lancet Report on the Sanitary Conditions at Londesborough Lodge

'The room occupied by his Royal Highness and his wife were separated from the dining and breakfast room by a narrow corridor. At the end of this corridor is a water closet, the door of which opens directly onto the Princess' bedroom. None of the 'Royal' rooms has any special or thorough ventilation. The bedroom occupied by His Royal Highness is of moderate size. It has a fireplace. A fire was kept up all day, but as this room is directly over the housekeeper's, it was found necessary to let it out at night. Into this room, the water closet opens directly, the single door does not fit tight. At the northern extremity of the main corridor is a front door, and close to this is a second water closet. It has a small window but also uses a ventilator in the ceiling. A plumber stated that 'This ventilator is in a poor state of repair.' However, this had been inspected by a contractor before the Royal visit and found to be acceptable. While there was no smell, the commissioners asked if this could be the source of an escape of dangerous emanations which had permeated the whole house?

The report concluded that Londesborough Lodge lies at the summit of an extended length of sewers with no openings for the escape of gas or relief of pressure. The drainage to the house placed in positions where inspected is impossible. A rat found under the floor, which had no doubt escaped from the drain and with the fires in the house gaslights etc., with closed doors, poor ventilation and a bad water clinic. It seems impossible to doubt that Londesborough Lodge is most definitely tainted. There is little smell, no apparent deposits in the drains, yet the faint and deadly influence could be at the core of the problem.

During the visit no less than twenty-eight people slept in the house. Eighteen servants. Ten guests and family members. Nine servants on the ground floor, the rest above. Before the Royal visit, the rooms had been occupied by other guests, who also became ill.

The Monday following the departure of the Prince of Wales and his guests the Earl of Chesterfield slept in the same room and stayed for one week.

*

The Lancet Report on the Sanitary Conditions at Sandringham

The commission was twofold, and in comparison, the Lancet commission reported that the sanitary condition at Sandringham Hall professed that 'the drainage is good, but the water supply bad.' Moreover, the analysis of Sandringham water points to the origin of the groom's attack, the water in the hall was of a particularly sorry state.

Furthermore, the British Medical Journal and the Lancet commissioners concluded that with regards to their investigation into the origin of the illness of The Prince of Wales and the Earl of Chesterfield that they were satisfied that both men caught the infection at Londesborough Lodge and the groom at Sandringham. The officials were of the view that the water at Londesborough Lodge was polluted, but further investigation would be required to determine the exact source of the contamination.

*

Understandably, Scarborough Corporation was not impressed with the Lancet's findings and commissioned their own architect's report which concluded that 'We have carefully examined the drains and cesspools both inside and out at the Lodge and we have found them to be perfect.'

The press was scathing in their response to this statement. The Manchester Evening News stating: 'The report commissioned by Scarborough Corporation and its findings is in our opinion a hasty one.

We have ourselves discovered that one of the architects who signed this statement admitted that there is one of the cesspools which was not examined, in fact, it had not been opened in years. If at all. This pit is most likely the source of the illness, as this cesspool received the drainage of five of the six closets.

Furthermore, this drain was in the basement, immediately below the cabinet of the bedroom occupied by the Prince of Wales, which opened into the Prince's bedchamber, which is connected by a 10ft pipe. These cesspools empty themselves into sewers which run into the sea.'

An independent source told the reporter that 'when the workmen had finished work on the present system of drainage at the Lodge, there was such a back-draft up the drain that it blew the candle out; it was so strong that it would have blown a dozen candles out.

Let us also consider, that in addition to the illness of the Prince of Wales and Lord Chesterfield, two other servants employed in the house also became ill with Typhoid Fever. Lord Chesterfield occupied this same room directly after the Prince, and this is the same room which has the infected drain directly beneath it.'

The reporter then went on to discredit the town of Scarborough itself stating, 'Scarborough is one of the worst drained towns in the country. The old town is simply a mass of middens and almshouses, mixed with bad stenches.

Moreover, the Royal party were shooting for a few days from Ayton to Willoughby, which is nothing more than low black swampy land five miles from Scarborough. A few years ago, Ayton was rampant with Typhoid Fever. According to medical reports, Scarborough has in the year 1871 never been entirely free of low fever. This distinguished party passed several times the disgusting public midden on Seamer Road, which is most offensive.

Recently, Scarborough has reported four deaths from Scarlet Fever. However, there has also been Typhoid Fever in the area surrounding Sandringham.

Taking all the evidence into account, the facts all point to the source of the illness to be from sewage poison at Scarborough, bearing in mind that Londesborough Lodge itself has all the worst faults which all breed poison. We conclude that without doubt, Scarborough is the cause of this typhoid infection.' (Manchester Times, Saturday 9th December 1871)

*

(7th December 1871) It seemed that after several nights of hallucinations that at last, the Prince was on the road to recovery, however when returning from a walk Princess Alexandra and Princess Alice found the Prince in a state of relapse. Sir Edward Jenner was called for, who after examining the Prince, sent an urgent telegram to the Queen proclaiming the Prince was far from well with a temperature of 104. The renowned doctor was most anxious. Once again, the Queen returned to Sandringham convinced that her precious firstborn son would die on the 14th December, the tenth anniversary of her husband's death.

Princess Alexandra was also sure that there was no hope for her adored husband, Bertie. As far as she was concerned, he was doomed.

Fearing the worst, the Queen entered her son's chambers on 14th December and was amazed to see him sat up in bed smiling, the fever had at last abated.

As the Prince began to recover, bulletins were posted outside Marlborough House much to the joy of the public. Queen Victoria in a letter to the press expressed her happiness at the touching sympathy exhibited to her son and members of the Royal family, which she exclaimed had left a sincere and heartfelt impression on her heart. A thanksgiving service was held, and individual coins issued in celebration of the Prince's recovery.

Good News at last. Crowds gather to read a bulletin from Marlborough House. (Illustrated London News)

In Yorkshire, a meeting was held at York chaired by the High Sherriff of the county Sir Henry Edwards Bart to congratulate the Queen on the recovery of the Prince of Wales. Noblemen and Gentlemen came from all over the three counties to represent all classes within their areas. The following form of address was written to the Queen.

To the Queen her most excellent Majesty.

'May it please your Majesty we, your Majesty's most faithful subjects of Yorkshire, beg humbly to offer her Majesty our congratulations upon the restoration to health of your Majesty's oldest son, the heir to the throne of this kingdom…

In assuring your Majesty of our loyal devotion. We fervently pray that you will reign over people who have enjoyed so much freedom, peace and happiness under your rule and that you may see your children and your children's children waiting happily in that course of duty in which your Majesty and your late consort have so conspicuously led the way.'

At this meeting, a letter was read out from Lord Londesborough expressing his great regret that he was not able to attend the meeting as he was prevented from doing so due to the indisposition of Lady Londesborough. He reminded the members present, that the East Riding had on three separate occasions hosted the Prince of Wales and that he had always left the warmest and kindest reflections.

The crowd gave a round of applause.

Grateful that her son had recovered. Queen Victoria and her officials planned to give Bertie some official role. Alas, perhaps due to his reputation this was not to be, and the philandering prince soon returned to his partying ways. Following his grave illness, the relationship he had with his wife improved. Furthermore, Queen Victoria after many years in the wilderness began to return to her official duties, her life and her family.

Scarborough in Queen Victoria's eyes was the root of the problem, and she blamed the town for the scare. She would never have a good word to say about the town and forbade her son and any member of the family from ever revisiting the town!

*

Scarborough's 'Famous' People

The town of Scarborough has produced not only many famous people but attracted many influential people to the town including the renowned Victorian photographer Oliver Sarony. The world-acclaimed actor Sir Ben Kingsley was born at Snainton, as was newsreader and journalist Selina Scott. Other notables include James Paul Moody (1887-1912) 6th officer on RMS Titanic and the only junior officer to die on the ill-fated ship, Joseph Rowntree, actor Charles Laughton, Sir George Cayley, the Sitwell family and many more. Unfortunately, we are not able to include them all in this book but will detail the influence that some of these people have had on the town.

*

Oliver Sarony, Photographer 1820-1879

Credit Ann Reniers.

Olivier François Xavier Sarony was born in Quebec in 1820 and moved to England in 1843. He eventually decided to settle in Scarborough after a brief spell in many Yorkshire towns including, Leeds, Bradford, and Doncaster. In Scarborough, Sarony commissioned architects John & David Petch to build him substantial photography studios of 98 rooms. At the time it was one of the most harmonious pieces of art in the town. Sarony bought the land from the South Cliff Company who placed restrictions on the use of the property, which were that the property had to be in keeping with the rest of the neighbourhood, could not be extended any higher than the original plans and the property were not be used as an inn, a beer or a boarding house. The gardens also had to be fenced off with iron railings.

Built-in the Lombardo-Venetian style, the building was divided into two, Gainsborough House and Vandyke House although from outside it looked like one large property. The lavishly decorated studio had been spared no expense and was surrounded by exquisite gardens and hedges that occupied a large square on the South Cliff. The entrance was on Oliver Street where two stone lions guarded a noble flight of steps which led to the door. Twenty-six carved figures said to represent Sarony's staff of talented artists, with a character of Sarony himself facing seaward with his tongue sticking out adorned the front of the property.

The reception room was striking with portraits of celebrated gentlemen and beautiful women. Sarony specialised in high-quality photographs, and he used the then-new carbon process, he also focussed on enlarging photographic portraits which he and his staff hand-finished in oil paints.

The studio employed an army of over 200 staff and was said to be the most extensive photographic studio in Europe. People flocked from all over the world to have their photographs taken at this famous studio and by one of the most celebrated photographers of the time.

Oliver Sarony was awarded a silver medal for bravery in 1861 for his part in the lifeboat disaster when he tried and failed to save the life of Mr Beauclerk. He did, however, retrieve his body from the sea.

Sarony also photographed HRH the Prince of Wales during his fateful visit to the town in 1871.

As a mark of respect to this renowned photographer's success Scarborough Corporation renamed this part of the South Cliff 'Sarony Square' in honour of this talented gentleman.

In its heyday, the studio turned over twenty thousand pounds and most of this incredible sum earned during the three-month tourist season. Sarony was by all accounts a kind and generous employer, so much so that on his 25th wedding anniversary the staff presented the couple with three vine-painted flower stands which they filled with fresh fruit.

Sadly, Oliver Sarony died in 1879, at the age of 59. He had diabetes and passed away from the effects of a paralytic stroke. The company continued for some time under the name of Sarony & Co-managed by Samuel Waind Fisher, the husband of Oliver's niece, Jennie, daughter of the New York photographer Napoleon Sarony. (Brother)

Seventeen months later Sarony's wife Elizabeth remarried a much younger man Thomas Dawes, who not only involved himself in the business but added the name Sarony to his surname. Elizabeth Sarony Dawes and her husband were living in Vandyke House.

The company continued, but by 1884 Gainsborough house had been offered for lease, as estate agents and auctioneers John Read & Co advertised for sale its entire contents, which they had bought from a Mr WS Caine MP who was leaving town. In 1891 it was occupied by a Dr Barker who ran The Retreat, a charitable organisation caring for the mentally ill (also in York). The Retreat stayed at Gainsborough House until 1902 and then moved on to Throxenby Hall, a property owned by Lord Londesborough.

By 1913 the business had moved to 17 St Nicholas Street, Scarborough and the property at Sarony Square fell into disrepair. In 1925 the Sarony business was bought by Ralph William Clarke, a court photographer and an artist. He kept the company going until he retired in 1960. The premises at St Nicholas Street was demolished to make room for the Town Hall extension.

Despite being advertised for sale suggesting different uses such as a hotel, school, public rooms etc, it seems that nobody was willing to take on the Gainsborough/Vandyke house building, and the restrictions previously put in place must have hindered any potential buyer. Scarborough Council bought the site, and the building was finally demolished in 1924 when it was intended to build houses, but instead, very sadly it was turned into tennis courts and eventually ended up as Albion Road/Oliver Street car park.

In the 1930s five houses opposite the demolished studio were turned into an 85-bedroom hotel called The Fairview, which continued in business until 1986 when the property was turned into 33 flats and sympathetically restored.

Thankfully, as a mark of respect to Oliver Sarony, the owners of Fairview Hotel preserved the only part of the history remaining of this most successful photographic studio and its entrepreneurial owner. They saved the plaster heads and erected them on the wall of the hotel where they remain to this day. A historical blue plaque dedicates the memory of this famous studio.

Oliver Sarony, his wife Elizabeth and her second husband are all buried in Dean Road Cemetery. Ironically, Beauclerk the man whose life Sarony tried to save in 1861 is buried in the next plot.

*

The Sitwell Family

Sir George Sitwell

The first mention of the Sitwell family is found in the record office in 1229 and shows that Simon 'Sitewel' of Ridgeway was heir to certain lands and tenements in Barlbro.' Lands, which his father Walter de Boys had held by feudal tenure before his death in Jerusalem. From that date on, the name of the Sitwell family is to be found amongst the higher classes of Yeomanry. The Sitwell's frequently filled the offices of the country's High Sheriffs and married into some of the oldest families in Derbyshire. In the reign of Elizabeth, I, the Sitwell name appeared amongst the gentry with Robert Sitwell of Stavely.

Francis Sitwell of Eckington, son, married Catherine Sacheverell daughter of one of the oldest families in Derbyshire and sister of William, who was the first orator in the House of Commons. William married Mary, the daughter of Lord Reresby of Thryberg, their daughter and heiress Frances Sitwell married John Hurt who changed his name to Sitwell.

In 1625, George Sitwell (1600–1667), High Sheriff of Derbyshire in 1653, built Renishaw Hall, a grand gothic house on the edge of Chesterfield, which became the ancestral family home of the Sitwell family.

The Sitwell's made their fortune in the 16/17th centuries from landowning and iron making, making nails and saws and exporting them to the West Indies and America. The English Civil war made the Sitwell family very wealthy indeed.

The first Baronet of the Sitwell family was Sir Sitwell Sitwell (1769-1811) a British politician and landowner. In honour of his grandfather, the second Baronet (1797–1853) George Sitwell named his son Sitwell (1820-1862) who by all accounts embraced life with enthusiasm. He even used his hounds to capture a Bengal Tiger which had escaped from a Sheffield menagerie in 1793.

Unfortunately, in the mid-nineteenth century, there were many incidents associated with this house including a fire, robbery and even the murder of the gamekeeper. Sir George Sitwell came close to bankruptcy. He auctioned the entire contents of the hall, including valuable paintings and even the timber in the surrounding woods. He retreated to Germany, where the cost of living was lower, but even then, he was too poor to afford a fire in winter. Renishaw might have been doomed, had it not been for the timely discovery of coal on the estate, and Sir George's descendants set about refilling the virtually empty house.

The 3rd Baronet, Sir Sitwell Reresby Sitwell (1820-1862) married Louisa Lucy Hely-Hutchinson in 1857. The couple had three children Florence Alice (1858-1930) and Sir George (1860-1943) and Blanche Tremayne born 1861. Sir George died after a short illness in 1863 and the age of 42. His son George became the third baronet at the age of two.

Following the death of her husband, Louisa moved the family to Scarborough. Tragedy struck again as her youngest daughter died not long after the move at the age of two and a half.

Initially, the family lived in a modest villa named' Sunnyside' on the corner of Royal Crescent but moved to Wood End in 1870. Louisa dedicated her life to charity work and founded the 'Red House' a home of hope for destitute girls, and a hospital at Kings Cliff.

Louisa's daughter Florence liked to write. Writing a diary which was published simultaneously with the journal of her aunt Georgina Caroline Sitwell who was born in 1824 reflecting on two generations of women. Georgina's diary depicted an England unspoilt by the Industrial Revolution with its smoke and grime of the chimneys and the hateful money-grabbing period which would descend on what was a green and pleasant land. Whereas in comparison, Florence's diary told of hypocrisy, slums, affluence and bad taste. An interesting contrast to the serenity of her aunt's replications. She also wrote a book entitled 'Daybreak' a story for girls. Florence never married. She spent her last year's in Warwickshire bedridden and died in 1930.

Sir George became an MP for Scarborough in 1885, and a year later married seventeen-year-old Ida Dennison third daughter of Lord and Lady Londesborough (Scarborough). The couple had only met on two previous occasions, but George knew she was the perfect match for him. Not because of her youth and outstanding beauty, but because of her pure 'blue blood' and her being a direct descent to the house of the Plantagenet.

The marriage took place at St George's, Hanover Square in London. The bridegroom showered his bride with jewels. Ida was ill-prepared for marriage and only three days later rushed home to her mother. She was instructed to return to her husband, still mindful that she had to contend with a man whose fixed ideas she would have to live with until her death in 1937.

The couple had three children Edith Louisa born 1887, Francis Osbert Sacheverell Sitwell, born 1892, and Sir Sacheverell Reresby Sitwell born 1887.

The Sitwell children all endured a questionable childhood in letters to her brothers Edith wrote: 'I do not believe there is another family in England like ours!' The children called their father 'Ginger- the horror, old beast' (though never to his face).

Lady Edith also declared 'I was unpopular with my parents from the moment I was born. My father ignored me, and my mother bullied me.' She recalls some of her earliest memories of her mother forcing her to wear a back brace to improve her posture and a nose truss to improve her looks. Another memory is of seventeen-year-old Edith been sent out into the town of Scarborough to pawn her mother's false teeth; she received ten shillings and five pence for them. Her mother was not impressed as Whisky was twelve shillings and sixpence a bottle. Poor Edith's nervous system she said, was ruined before the age of ten.

Their father George lost his Parliamentary seat for the second time in 1895 and turned his attention to writing unfathomable books such as 'The history of the fork' and other obscure titles. He even went as far as to have the cows on his estate stencilled in a blue willow pattern so that they would be more attractive.

He spent most of his time as a recluse living on roast chicken which he ate alone in full evening dress. He also invented some strange devices such as a pistol for shooting wasps, a musical toothbrush and a synthetic egg made of smoked meat and rice. He attempted to sell the egg to Selfridges, barging into their offices without an appointment declaring. 'I am Sir George Sitwell; this is my egg!'

Much to the embarrassment of his sons, he tried to pay their school fees at Eton with home-grown fayre, and he spent most of his time sending letters to the taxman. In his later years, he was supported by his dedicated butler Henry Moat who travelled with him throughout Europe.

Avoiding the Inland Revenue, Sir George moved to Italy and in 1909 bought a castle just outside Florence named Castello di

Montegufoni where he spent the rest of his life renovating and decorating it. Sir George died in Locarno, Switzerland in 1943.

Lady Ida Sitwell

The once beautiful Ida had allegedly turned into a vicious drunken bully with questionable morals, who directed most of her anger on her daughter.

She was hopelessly extravagant, childlike with money, and unacquainted with business matters. Ida's debt problems soon spiralled out of control, and she found herself in severe debt and the subject of court proceedings. On one occasion a case was heard against her at the Bloomsbury Court in London for unpaid debts from a boot and shoe supplier amounting to over twenty-five pounds. At the hearing, her husband Sir George stated that he had discovered his wife's debts and had advanced her a loan of two thousand seven hundred pounds, which he paid directly to the Scarborough tradesmen. Also, he increased her allowance to four hundred a year and took a lien on her jewellery. The case was dismissed.

Her problems were not over, as, in 1912, Ida found herself the subject of a much-publicised almighty scandal, when she was accused of conspiracy to defraud. Ida was forced to raise money from an insurance company as her debts at that time were two thousand pounds but her income only four hundred per annum. Her husband flatly refused to bail her out again.

Ida became acquainted with a Mr Field, who she had met at the Curzon Hotel in London. Field told her that he could help her raise funds, but that he wasn't a moneylender, but a moneylender's tout. Ida trusted Field entirely and signed anything he put in front of her. Field got Ida to draw two discounted bills of three thousand pounds each which were to be repaid within three months. They were both dishonoured.

These bills were backed by an innocent lady called Miss Dobbs of Streatham who had never seen the bills and had never met Lady Ida Sitwell.

On this occasion, the Judge stood the case down as the plaintiff was unwell and gave Miss Dobbs the opportunity to have the case heard by a jury. Unfortunately for Ida, this was not the end of the case as in 1915 it resurfaced and was heard at the Old Bailey.

At the trial, the defence called her husband Sir George as a witness, where he stated that his wife had expected him or her brother Lord Londesborough to pay her debts, but they refused to on this occasion, as he had already done so on a previous occasion.

After a seven-day trial, Ida and the dubious moneylender Field were found guilty of fraud. Field received an 18-month prison sentence.

Ida's lawyers pleaded with the judge for leniency, stressing that Ida was in 'a grave condition of health.' She was examined by the chief medical officer who found her fit, but neurotic. The judge sentenced her to three months in Holloway Prison and commented that if it had not been for her state of health, it would have been much longer. Ida, upon hearing the sentence almost fainted but managed to conceal her feelings. She walked down the steps to the cells flanked by two wardens.

Ida died in 1937 in a London nursing home. Her daughter did not attend the funeral because of her displeasure with her parents during her childhood. Furthermore, Lady Edith never forgave her father for not settling her mother's debts during the court case and subjecting the family to such public condemnation.

*

The Talented Sitwell Children

Despite their parent's disregard, Edith, Osbert and Saucherville all became gifted writers. Edith a fragile, sensitive girl became a poet and an author. She never married, but Edith's home in Bayswater was always open to London's poetic circle, to whom she was unfailingly generous and helpful. Edith retired to Renishaw with her brother Osbert and his companion, David Horner. She took to wearing a turban and sizeable clunky jewellery (she said she wore the turban as she could not do a thing with her hair). She liked to dress in wild mediaeval clothes, that gave her a striking resemblance to Elizabeth I. Edith was a poetic genius, one of her plays 'Fanfare for Elizabeth' reached Hollywood and was scripted for a film.

Initially, Edith wanted to be a musician but decided that music was not for her and joined a group of young writers. Soon her brothers joined in, and they started a magazine called 'Wheels'. The literary genius of the Sitwell children had begun.

Osbert and Saucherville were equally talented in writing, poetry and novels, and Osbert an autobiography. The siblings were known as the spearhead of the 'Avant-Garde' who attracted many creative and talented people to their inner circle.

*

The Cayley Family of Brompton-by-Sawdon

The Cayley family were residents at Brompton Hall (Brompton-by-Sawdon) from 1604 when Edward Cayley the father of the first Baronet purchased the house and made it the family seat until they vacated it in c.1930. (Yorkshire Post & Leeds Intelligencer, 6th April 1934)

The first Baronet was Sir William Cayley (1610-1681) who married Dorothy St. Quintin, descended from a family with many memorials in the church of nearby Harpham. The Cayley's were a family of great antiquity who originated from Norfolk, where Hugh de Cailly was Lord of Owby. The surname Cayley derives from the town name of Cailly in Normandy, reflecting the fact that William the Conqueror rewarded his faithful followers with English property and other rights.

In medieval times, the most powerful Cayley was Thomas de Cailly, Lord of Buckenham in Norfolk (c.1282-1316). Thomas inherited very vast estates (which alas passed out of the Cayley family soon after his death) and married the daughter of Walter de Norwich, who was Chief Baron of the Exchequer – roughly equivalent to the Chancellor of the Exchequer today – from 1311 to 1317 when he resigned on health grounds. Thomas de Cailly's mother was Emma de Tattershall, a great-granddaughter of William de Albini, 4th Earl of Arundel. It is that William d'Albini's great-grandfather, another William d'Albini and first Earl of Arundel (c.1109-1176), to whom our tale relates. (Michael Cayley, 26, January 2018)

William de Albini is the main character regarding the peculiarity of the Cayley (Cailly) crest. After the death of King Henry, I of England in

1135, William d'Albini became engaged to Henry's widow, Adeliza de Louvain. He went in pursuance of her commands to seek for Glory in the French wars. While on this chivalrous expedition the Queen Dowager of France fell in love with him, and on his confessing his engagement to Adeliza her majesty became so enraged that she contrived his destruction by mean of a lion pit. William de Albini did not fear the lion, and he attacked and killed the creature and tore out its tongue. Since that time the crest of the Cayley's represents the demi-lion rampant without its tongue, grasping the battle-axe with which it was slain.

Credit Michael Cayley

The Cayley Baronetcy is an old one and was created by Charles II in 1661 for services rendered to his father, Charles I in the English Civil Wars, who in fact had knighted him in 1641.

Sir George Cayley, the 6th Baronet, was a man of considerable eminence in the scientific world as a practical experimentalist and an inventive mechanic. Born in 1773 at Paradise House, Scarborough, the only son of Sir Thomas Cayley (1732-92) and Isabella Seton (c.1745-1828) he had four sisters and was schooled in York, before receiving private tutoring by two non-conformist ministers, George Walker and George Cadogan Morgan.

Sir George inherited the Baronetcy in 1792 on the death of his father. He was eighteen. He also inherited the family estate centred on Brompton Hall which was his primary residence. He also spent a lot of time at a further house in central London. He married Miss Sarah Walker, daughter of one of his tutors, in July 1795. Together they had a large family.

Sir George was an intelligent man, with varying interests in engineering, but his real passion was in aeronautics. In 1796, he built a model helicopter. Furthermore, he drew attention to the possibility of the navigation of balloons, while at the same time pointing out that the steam-engine would be too heavy for this purpose. Cayley led the way in aeronautics, and one engine he designed became the prototype for one later patented by Ericsson in America. As early as 1807, Sir George had published an article in Nicholson's Journal giving an account of an air engine, which is understood to be the earliest on record.

Sir George patented this engine which included some improvements. Ericsson showed an interest in his designs and had Sir George's patent did not expire until some two months before John Ericsson's engine was marketed, thus, Ericsson's engine would have been an infringement of this patent. (York Herald 12 February 1853)

Most of Sir George's experiments were worked on in an eighteenth-century workshop at Brompton Hall. By 1853, John Appleby, a coachman to the Cayley's was ordered to 'pilot' a glider. He was petrified and quickly handed in his notice saying, 'Please Sir George, I wish to give notice! I was hired to drive and not to fly!'

Moreover, together with his incredible inventions, Sir George was also briefly a Whig MP for Scarborough, the first chairman of the York Mechanics' Institute and he also originated a cottage allotment system for his tenants, whereby fourteen cottages on the Cayley estate were given sixteen acres of land to grow crops. Each cottage could keep a cow. The rent for each cottage was less than ten pounds per annum.

Sir George Cayley died on 15th December 1857, aged almost 84, at Brompton Hall and is buried in the family vault at nearby All Saints Church. He is considered as the father of aeronautics, a remarkable inventor who paved the way for the Wright Brothers, whose first powered flight was 50 years later. His work is well respected, and NASA and many other scientific institutions acknowledge the importance of Cayley's work.

*

The ninth Baronet, Sir George Everard Cayley, a keen sportsman and one-time president of Scarborough Cricket Club, lived beyond his means. Unfortunately, he was declared bankrupt in 1907 with considerable debts. Following his death in 1917, his son Kenelm became the tenth Baronet. Sir Kenelm became a prisoner-of-war in the war and reached the rank of Major.

Like his father before him, and with the economic climate of the country, and despite spending considerable sums of money on massive improvements to the estate in circa 1947, Sir Kenelm found it challenging to make ends meet. This resulted in his selling much of the village in 1953 the Inland Revenue the vigorously pursued Sir Kenelm (Yorkshire Post), and as a result, he moved to Jersey as a tax exile later in the 1950s. He was only allowed back into the United Kingdom for ninety days in each tax year and was separated from his wife (his wife did not live with him in Jersey) and family and the village of Brompton they loved; the family could not settle on the Island.

The Hall which had been empty for over three years was leased in 1934 to Hotel Services Ltd and became a fashionable hotel called Brompton Hall Hotel. In 1950, the Hall was sold again for twenty-five thousand pounds and became a special needs school for one-hundred children, now run by North Yorkshire County Council. By 1952, the rest of the Brompton estate was offered for sale. The sale produced fifty-eight thousand pounds and a few lots did not sell, thereby remaining as tenanted houses in Brompton.

W.M. Rhodes

Illustrated Particulars, Plan and Conditions of Sale of

THE BROMPTON ESTATE
Total 1572 Acres

GREEN FARM - 209 Acres   HOME FARM - 114 Acres

Woodlands, Estate Yard, two Sites, Parkland and Accommodation Land
in all 428 Acres

VACANT OR EARLY POSSESSION

Also an Excellent Investment including
Five Farms-109 to 396 acres.   Five Smallholdings.
House and General Store, Butcher's Shop, House and Garage Premises.
Several Lots of Accommodation Land and Building Sites.
Thirty-two cottages in Brompton Village.

PRODUCING ❷2,536 PER ANNUM

Thank you to Michael Cayley and Vivian Bairstow for their help and contribution to this section.

*

233

The Titanic Connection Sir Edward Harland

Sir Edward Harland. (WikiCommons Licence)

Scarborough claims two connections to the Titanic. The first is the owner of the shipyard Harland & Wolff, the shipyard responsible for the building of the Titanic. The second is James P Moody who was the youngest officer on the vessel.

Mr Edward Harland who was born in 1831 at a house where Marks & Spencer now stands, the 6th child from a family of ten. His parents were both mechanically minded. His father was a medical doctor, a Justice of the Peace, and Mayor of Scarborough on three occasions. His mother came from a landed family in Goathland who also displayed an interest in mechanical engineering, so much so that the children's nursery became more of a workshop than filled with traditional toys and games.

As a boy Harland showed considerable mechanical talent, preferring to spend his time making models of watermills and engines. He attended Scarborough Grammar school and worked at WM Tindall shipbuilding yard where he gained considerable knowledge and helped with the building of East Indiaman ships.

At the age of twelve, he was sent away to Edinburgh Academy where he spent two years receiving classical training. His father wanted him to be a barrister, but Harland was adamant that his talents were best suited to engineering. At the age of fifteen, he went to work for Messrs Robert Stephenson & Co engineers in Newcastle.

In 1850, he entered a competition promoted by the Duke of Northumberland to find the best model for a new lifeboat (the design of lifeboats up to this date were unsatisfactory). Edward Harland designed a metal lifeboat, propelled by a screw at each end. Harland's design did not win, but his model was later adopted into shipbuilding.

Harland made rapid advances in shipbuilding design and engineering and moved to Belfast as manager of Queens Island shipbuilding yard, the owner Robert Hickson retired, and Harland seized the opportunity to purchase his own yard. Mr Gustav Wilhelm Wolff, who had been Harland's assistant, became his partner. Harland & Wolff were formed and soon became one of the most successful shipbuilders in the world, securing contracts far and wide, including White Star who was responsible for the ill-fated 'unsinkable' ship the Titanic.

In 1885, Harland was granted a knighthood and a baronetcy. He also served as MP for Belfast. Sir Edward Harland died in 1895 many years before the fateful voyage of the Titanic.

*

James P Moody

James P Moody was born at 17 Granville Road, Scarborough on 21st August 1887 to John Henry Moody and Evelyn Louise Lammin. His grandfather had been town clerk, and his father a solicitor at Messrs Turnbull, Graham & Moody and a member of the town council. James was educated at Mr Sanderson's private school in Scarborough then took nautical training in London where he gained a master's degree. He joined the White Star company where he was a 6th officer for the liner The Oceanic. He transferred to the Titanic at the last minute after receiving a telegram from White Star ordering him to move ships, not even his family were aware that their son was aboard the first sailing of this ship's fateful voyage. The first the family knew that their son was on board was from a visit of a press reporter.

As a 6th officer, the pay was not good at only thirty-seven pounds a year but compensated with the use of his own cabin. On his first day, Moody inadvertently saved the lives of six crewmen who were late for their duties; Moody closed the last gangway, thus sparing them from the unknown disaster which followed.

The duties of the 6th officer was to stand by the Captain always. On that fateful day, Moody did just that. He took the call from the crow's nest asking, 'what do you see?' answering, 'Iceberg right ahead.' It was Moody who entered the time of the collision in the ship's log.

The second-fifth officers took charge of the lifeboats, and all left the ship to help the passengers. The Captain's duty was to stand by his ship until the last command was given (when nothing more can be done). 'Every man for himself and God for us all' is the motto. Until the last moment comes, the junior officer's duty was to stand by his Captain, pass commands, and be steadfast unto death. This act of bravery is just what the twenty-four-year-old brave man did. He saved others by putting their lives before his own. He could not save himself.

Following the disaster, first reports suggested that Moody was safe, then his name was reported as J Pelloody. His family were unaware of their brave son's fate. Much appreciation is bestowed on Moody for his courageous actions. Moody's body was never recovered, but he is remembered in Woodland Cemetery where the inscription states. 'Greater love hath no man than this, that a man lay down his life for his friends.' (John: 15:13. KJV)

R.I.P.

*

Charles Laughton

Public Domain

Hollywood actor Charles Laughton was born in Scarborough. The eldest of three sons to Robert and Eliza Laughton whose family had invested borrowed money into running The Victoria Hotel opposite Scarborough Railway Station, a business started by Laughton's grandfather. The couple worked so hard that soon they had enough money to buy The Pavilion Hotel on the opposite side of the station.

From an early age, Charles knew that he wanted to be an actor. He studied at Scarborough College and the Jesuit public school Stonyhurst where at the age of fifteen he made his acting debut, playing an innkeeper.

Laughton's mother wanted him to get a proper career and insisted that he leave school to train at Claridge's Hotel in London to take over the family business. In 1917, like many other young men his age, Laughton was called to do his duty, a calling that left him both physically and mentally damaged.

Following the death of his father in 1924, Laughton returned to London to study at the Royal Academy of Dramatic Arts, where he gained much acclaim. Laughton met the actress Elsa Lanchester in London, and they married in 1929 at London Register Office. The couple did not have any children. Lanchester in her autobiography described their marriage as 'A kind of Domestic Limited Company.' Despite their 'reported differences' the couple were married 33 years.

Laughton was considered a great actor, but perhaps not 'handsome' enough (back then) to play a lead role. Instead, he played the role of terrors and tyrants such as the role of Quasimodo in the Hunchback of Notre Dame. He received an Oscar for his portrayal of Henry VIII; the film was an unexpected success costing only sixty-five thousand pounds to make with ticket sales of over seven hundred and fifty pounds. Charles Laughton was paid just one thousand pounds for his performance. This role paved the way for more films including Jamaica Inn and The Barrets of Wimpole Street.

Charles Laughton returned to Scarborough in 1936 at the opening of the Odeon (now Stephen Joseph Theatre) as his mother and brother also attended the opening. He died at his home in California in 1962 from kidney cancer; he is buried at Forest Lawn Cemetery in California.

The family were well known for their splendid hospitality, food and the décor of their hotels, which included The Pavilion, The Royal and Holbeck Hall. Brothers Tom and Frank both thrived in the hotel business and prided themselves on making their guests feel like millionaires during their holiday. Thomas Laughton was a shrewd businessman and a prolific art collector. A sale of his art collection was sold at Sotheby's for almost one hundred and four thousand pounds including a portrait by Constable of his sleeping wife painted in 1827, which fetched three thousand seven hundred pounds and another seven thousand pounds named 'Contradiction' painted by Richard Dadd when he was in 'Bedlam' hospital after murdering his father and encouraged to paint as a therapy treatment by his doctor.

The Royal Hotel continues to this day and is considered one of Scarborough's best hotels. The Pavilion Hotel closed and was demolished in 1973. The Holbeck Hotel suffered a well-publicised landfall and slipped into the sea in 1993, while some guests were having breakfast.

Ramsdale Valley Bridge

Scarborough Old Photographs. (Facebook)

Back in 1849, Scarborough Corporation permitted Mr Robert Williamson to build a bridge to connect Ramsdale Valley to the rest of Scarborough. The Corporation agreed to impose a rent to Mr Williamson of five pounds per annum for a lease of 999 years. Time lapsed, and the idea was forgotten until an unfortunate accident with Leman Bridge at York brought the suggestion back to the forefront. Residents soon raised opposition to the erection of this bridge, which would take quite a chunk of the Plantation away, a beautiful public pleasure ground known as Love Lane, leaving only a narrow thoroughfare passage to it between a 10ft wall, which would deem this ancient walk unattractive to visitors.

The council argued that the loss of a section of the Plantation would be compensated by connection to that side of the valley with the rest of Scarborough. Protestors were still not convinced stating that in their opinion the Corporation had in effect alienated the town to benefit a private company for whom this bridge was built. Furthermore, it came to light that Mr Woodall had offered at advantageous terms a field at the side of the valley which could have accommodated this bridge, and therefore not encroached on the Plantation at all, this was to be on the proviso that the bridge would be toll-free and available to all. Unfortunately, the Corporation was unable to secure funding, so the project was offered to a private company. Mr Woodall declined this same offer to Mr Williamson and his Limited Company, so Mr Woodall sold his land privately. A vote put to the members with the result in favour of the Corporation and the construction of the Ramsdale Valley Bridge commenced.

The first steps taken were by Mr Alexander Taylor, the borough surveyor who staked out the ground showing the centre at the end of the road to be taken by the bridge from Love Lane and Belmont Road. The bridge was initially intended as Lendal Bridge York, but it collapsed there and was brought to Scarborough where it was erected upside down.

Originally, to cross the bridge there was a half-penny toll. It opened on 1st July 1865, to a vast crowd who had come out in droves to witness this spectacular occasion. The ceremony was represented by every public body in the town

As transport progressed and more people owned cars the bridge soon became inadequate, the bridge was far too narrow, and the structure was widened and strengthened in 1911.

Not long after in 1928 the bridge was completely rebuilt and opened to the public on 27th July 1929 by Mrs Ashley wife of the minister of Transport amidst much pomp and ceremony.

Credit Paul Thomas

There have been many reported tragedies and accidents related to this bridge over the years. May those who lost their lives R.I.P.

Author's own collection

Marine Drive

Marine Drive 1908 (The Tatler 1908)

The Woods and Forest department granted a licence for Scarborough to build a marine drive which would join the north and the south bays. The Town Council sought permission from the owners and ratepayers to consent to them borrowing seventy thousand pounds for the proposed building works which would employ many men.

The foundation stone was laid in 1897 and timed to coincide with the sixty-year reign of Queen Victoria. The contractors were under contract, and for every day over the scheduled completion time, there would be a five-pound penalty. In fairness, bad weather and severe storms delayed the building for some time when 100 feet of the wall blew away. The cost of the building ran over budget considerably.

SCARBOROUGH: NEW MARINE DRIVE.
LAYING THE LAST BLOCK.

Author's own collection

After seven years the final block out of a total of over 1500 blocks weighing from 2-9 tons of the four-mile-long wall, was laid by Scarborough's Mayoress, Mrs Morgan. At long last the Marine Drive, one of the finest, if not the finest stretch of drives in the kingdom, neared completion.

After much deliberation on who would facilitate the official opening of the drive, the honour was undertaken by the Duke and Duchess of Connaught in August 1908 accompanied by Princess Patricia.

The toll of two-pence per person for both motorists and pedestrians levied, but this was reduced to one-pence in 1934 following complaints from visitors.

*

Hairy Bob's Cave

There is a cave carved into the rock on the north side of the bay. The origins of this cave are open to debate. Some say that the cave is a 'folly' devised to attract tourists, while others say that it was used as a storeroom for tools for the men working on the construction of Marine Drive. Another theory is that a man called 'Hairy Bob' lived there. He sold Yellowstone around the town and had fallen out with his wife, therefore he moved into the cave.

An interesting theory is that Bob was a local drunk and constantly in trouble with the law. One day he found himself in trouble and taken to the Castle jail on the assumption that once he sobered up, he would be released. The day after a sober Bob still not happy with the two guards cursed them declaring that God would not take kindly to their actions. Later that night lightning struck the Castle, and the two guards were killed instantly. The only survivor was Hairy Bob who was found in his prison in a cave at the bottom of the cliff.

*

King Richard III House

ANCIENT HOUSE OF KING RICHARD III.

I t is reputed that King Richard III stayed at the house during the summer of 1484. He visited Scarborough to assemble a fleet against an expected invasion from Henry Tudor (Henry VII). The house has borne his name ever since.

The house was owned by antique dealer Mr E Booth-Jones who together with his wife and two children all perished on the Lusitania when it was struck by a German submarine. The house sold in 1917 for seven hundred and forty pounds to Mr E Booth-Jones' brother-in-law

Mr Burroughs. The property has had many uses from an antique shop, café and a restaurant.

Northstead Manor & Peasholm Park

Author's own collection

The lake at Peasholm holds significant interest as during excavations the foundations of a square Norman tower were discovered, together with a fireplace in herringbone pattern tiling which was like the one in Scarborough Castle.

The history of this manor house and the Northstead and Peasholm Estate is rather obscure as it seems to represent the earlier Hatterboard although neither place is mentioned in the Domesday Book.

We do know that 'the Manor of Northstead' consisted of a medieval manor house surrounded by farms and fields. Originally, the estate bordered to the north side of Scarborough following the line of Peasholm Beck. The estate passed to the ownership of the Crown during the reign of Richard III (1483–1485). (Wikipedia) At the beginning of Elizabeth's reign, the Northstead had a 'parlour', an old chamber reached by wooden stairs, and 'a lowe house under it' unfit for habitation. The manor house was at one time occupied by the shepherd of Sir Richard Cholmley, but the house became beyond repair and collapsed. Adjoining was an old decayed barn and the walls of other houses, which shortly afterwards fell, and an old chapel. Sir Richard Cholmley, the lessee of Edward VI, used the timber of these decayed buildings to build further buildings. (British History Online)

Mr George Blackett Rawlings owned land known as Rawlings field. He, his wife and ten children lived at Peasholm House. Mr Rawlings and his family had for many years owned the bathing machines on the north and south bay. Mr Rawlings died in March 1916 at the age of 63. Rawlings field sold to the Corporation at a minimum cost. Additional land was known as 'Tucker's Field' a neglected area occupied with piggeries and allotments with a stream passing through it which emptied itself into Peasholm Gap, was also acquired.

Later, in 1921 Scarborough Corporation bought the Northstead land, but not the Lordship of the manor, which is owned by the crown. The reason for retaining the Lordship is that technically, an MP is not allowed to resign – the only ways out of the Commons without losing an election are to die, be expelled, or to become disqualified. Therefore, one option MPs can use to be disqualified is by taking the position of The Steward and Bailiffs of the Chiltern Hundreds, and of the Manor of Northstead – two nominal titles which bar someone from being an MP. (British History Online)

In 1839, the land and Peasholm House was offered for lease;

NORTHSTEAD, near SCARBOROUGH, YORKSHIRE. TO be LET on LEASE, for the Term of Twenty-one Years, from the 11th day of October, 1839, a very VALUABLE ESTATE, belonging to her Majesty, called the NORTHSTEAD ESTATE, situate in the township of Newby, in the parish of Scalby, in the North Riding of the county of York, about half a mile from the celebrated watering place and borough town of Scarborough, adjoining to the Sea at Scarborough North Sands, and extending westward, adjoining the township of Falsgrave; the turnpike road from Scarborough to Whitby passing through the property, which contains 513A. 3R. 6P., and will be let by Tender by the Commissioners of her Majesty's Woods, Forests, Land Revenues, Works, and Buildings, on TUESDAY the 6th day of August, 1839, in Five Lots; viz.—

Lot 1. A MESSUAGE, called Peaseholme House, with barn, outbuildings, and meadow and pasture lands adjoining thereto, containing 41A. 2R. 4P.

Lot 2. Several Closes of Meadow, Pasture, and Arable LAND, within a ring fence, containing together 114A. 0R. 12P.

Lot 3. Several Closes of Meadow, Pasture, and Arable LAND, lying in a ring fence, containing together 107A. 3R. 14P.

Lot 4. Several Closes of Meadow, Pasture, and Arable LAND, lying in a ring fence, containing together 98A. 2R. 14P.

Lot 5. Several Closes of Meadow, Pasture, and Arable LAND, within a ring fence, containing together 151A. 3R. 2P.

The Estate is charged with annual payments amounting to 30l. 12s. 10d. in lieu of all tithes, which sums are to be paid by the Lessee of Lot 2.

Sealed Tenders for Leases may be addressed to the Commissioners of Woods, &c., under cover to the Right Honourable the Chief Commissioner, Office of Woods, &c. London, on or before the 6th day of August next, when the Tenders will be opened, and the highest offer for each Lot accepted, provided the same be not less than a sum to be named by the Commissioners, and inserted in a paper to be previously sealed up and opened at the same time with the Tenders, and provided the person making the same can give sufficient assurance or security, to the satisfaction of the Board, for payment of the rent offered, and for the due performance of the covenants to be inserted in the Lease, and in default thereof such Tender or Proposal will be rejected. Benjamin Waterworth, of Peaseholme House, will show the Premises; and printed Specifications and Conditions, with Plans annexed, may be had at the Talbot Inn, Scarborough; of Mr. Bower, Smeathalls, near Ferry Bridge; of Mr. Blacket, Stokesby; of Messrs. Heap and Appleby, solicitors, Scarborough; and at the Office of Woods, Forests, Land Revenues, Works and Buildings, Whitehall, London.

Office of Woods, London, 2d July, 1839.

Hull Packet July 1839.

Sir George Cawley of Brompton Hall took the lease mainly for political reasons. British History online records 'The scheme was suggested by Edward Cayley (relative) who considered the estate to provide a 'means of accommodation to many persons in Scarbro' and

... such influence as landed property naturally gives.' A guarantee fund was to be set up to defend Sir George against loss. The scheme was to be short-lived. Writing in 1852 Sir George says, "an honest split of opinion has however now occurred between the Whig Mulgrave party and myself" and wonders how to extract himself from the agreement.'

Another Liverpool of the East.

In 1845, plans for the land at Peasholm was put forward by George Hudson Esq, MP which was to build a new harbour and docks at Low Peasholm on the north side of Scarborough. Mr Hudson committed fifty thousand pounds to the scheme and a colleague a further ten thousand pounds. (Newcastle Chronicle, November 1845) The plan did not come to fruition, and the scheme was abandoned.

*

Peasholm & Northstead Manor Park

The post of borough's engineer was advertised in the press in 1896; 129 applicants applied, and the post given to thirty-year-old Harry W Smith at a salary of three hundred pounds per year. Smith was responsible for transforming much of Scarborough, including the Town Hall, Shuttleworth Gardens. Smith had a passion for exploiting natural beauty and planting trees. The development of Peasholm captures his outstanding ability and his creativity. Many considered his plans lavish and unnecessary and dubbed it 'the borough engineer's baby'. His vision for Peasholm was to excavate the swamp around Peasholm Beck and transform the stream into a lake. Around the lake, he would lay paths and flower beds, and build a boathouse, café and a bridge which would be in the Japanese style; the whole effect would be a willow pattern.

Scarborough's Lord and Lady Mayoress Mr and Mrs Good accompanied by dignitaries from the Corporation officially opened Peasholm Park and lake on 22nd June 1912. This day was a busy time for the town as later that same afternoon the Lord and Lady Mayoress also opened a new promenade, public shelters, bathing bungalows, together with the official opening of South Cliff Golf Club.

Further additions to the Park were made from time to time including the Bandstand, Waterfall and Pagoda, Miniature Golf Course together with several Chinese and Oriental statues and ornaments including the lions which were to guard the steps to the bridge and purchased by the Corporation from Kirby Misperton Hall.

*

The Miniature Railway

One of the main additional attractions was the miniature railway which lined Peasholm to Scalby Mills. The railway was popular with visitors and locals. It had all the features of a normal railway including tunnels, bridges and signal boxes. The trains were to scale of the LNER's Gresley engine, but instead of steam, the train was driven by a 26 BHP diesel engine. The miniature railway opened on the 25th May 1931, and its first passenger was Scarborough's, Mayor Ald. J W Butler who collected his ticket from Peasholm ticket office where he was presented with a peaked cap, an oil can and a sweat rag.

The train was so successful taking over five-thousand pounds in its first year of opening that the Corporation purchased a further train. Unfortunately, only a year after opening the railway had a serious accident when the trains collided killing one driver and injuring thirty-nine passengers. An inquiry followed and the 'system' blamed for the accident recommending that the council installed a second track to avoid another head-on collision.

July 1932 Illustrated London News.

A similar accident happened in 1948 when a collision occurred when the south-bound train, which had just left the double track at the beach station as it met the other train as it rounded the bend. A visitor described the sound of the collision as being 'just like a bomb going off.' (Yorkshire Post, 24th August 1948) Fortunately, no one was killed, but a mother and her son were trapped underneath, and both had fractured legs. Nine other people were treated at the scene with minor injuries.

The attraction closed during the war years but gained another function as a place for the Royal Naval School of Music to store their musical instruments while operating from the nearby Forbreak Hotel. On 30th March 2007, the operation of the line was formally taken over by the North Bay Railway Company Limited. Previously it had been owned and operated by Scarborough Borough Council. (Wikipedia)

*

The Open-Air Theatre

Author's own collection

Considered Scarborough's greatest entertainment project, the open-air theatre opened in July 1932, by the Lord Mayor of London to a packed house with all the six-thousand seats taken. The first production of Merrie England was such a success that production was expanded to include the cricket festival. The theatre continues to be busy and attracts acts from all over the world.

*

Hotels and Public Houses

Scarborough boasts many excellent hotels and public houses, and it is impossible to name them all. This book mentions the Royal, Pavilion and Holbeck Hall Hotel above, so here we will concentrate on a few more.

One of the oldest inns is the grade II listed Newcastle Packet. The original timber-framed house is believed to have been an H plan with jettied gabled wings facing the street. Academic research suggests that this house dated to the late fifteenth or early sixteenth century. The timber framing is like buildings in York dated circa 1500 and the inn is said to be partially constructed from an old ship's timber. The medieval house is believed to have survived intact until around 1725 when a new front was added to the centre and west wing, at which time the building served as the Post House. From 1830 this part of the house was a public-house, and the eastern part used as a shop. In 1898-9 the centre and west wing were rebuilt by the local architect Frank Tugwell, incorporating the surviving timbers from the original house, and in 1920 the east wing was rebuilt and incorporated into the public-house. During this reconstruction a fragment of the old town wall was unearthed, together with signage on a part of the ancient brickwork one with the name Justicia and another Cybele. It seems that this inn was at one time used as the offices of justice where all tolls and customs were paid and is said to have been a half-bow shot from the fort. The sign of Justicia represents the goddess of justice taking the toll for the fish- wives basket, while Cybele was the daughter of Justicia and offered the vestal fire in her mother's honour. (Leeds Mercury 1903)

Breweries

The first established brewery in Yorkshire was founded in 1691 by the Nesfield family known originally as Castle Road Brewery, then Newfield's Brewery. Following the death of George Nesfield in 1919, the business was offered for sale, which included thirty-three public houses from all around the area including Scarborough, Filey and Robin Hood's Bay. The buildings and business were bought by Messrs Moore & Robson of Hull for the sum of eighty-thousand pounds.

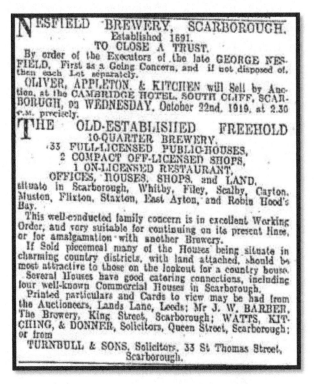

NESFIELD BREWERY, SCARBOROUGH.
Established 1691.
TO CLOSE A TRUST.

By order of the Executors of the late GEORGE NES-FIELD, First as a Going Concern, and if not disposed of, then each Lot separately.

OLIVER, APPLETON, & KITCHEN will Sell by Auc-tion, at the CAMBRIDGE HOTEL, SOUTH CLIFF, SCAR-BOROUGH, on WEDNESDAY, October 22nd, 1919, at 2.30 P.M. precisely.

THE OLD-ESTABLISHED FREEHOLD
10-QUARTER BREWERY,
33 FULL-LICENSED PUBLIC-HOUSES,
2 COMPACT OFF-LICENSED SHOPS,
1 ON-LICENSED RESTAURANT,
OFFICES, HOUSES, SHOPS, and LAND,
situate in Scarborough, Whitby, Filey, Scalby, Cayton, Muston, Flixton, Staxton, East Ayton, and Robin Hood's Bay.

This well-conducted family concern is in excellent Working Order, and very suitable for continuing on its present lines, or for amalgamation with another Brewery.

If Sold piecemeal many of the Houses being situate in charming country districts, with land attached, should be most attractive to those on the lookout for a country house.

Several Houses have good catering connections, including four well-known Commercial Houses in Scarborough.

Printed particulars and Cards to view may be had from the Auctioneers, Lands Lane, Leeds; Mr J. W. BARBER, The Brewery, King Street, Scarborough; WATTS, KIT-CHING, & DONNER, Solicitors, Queen Street, Scarborough; or from

TURNBULL & SONS, Solicitors, 33 St Thomas Street, Scarborough.

There was also the Scarborough & Whitby Brewery, which consolidated four breweries including Scarborough Brewing Company, Old Brewery Scarborough, with Corner & Readman and Marine Parade Brewery (Whitby). Concentration for the brewing was in Scarborough where production continued until 1953 when the company was sold to John J Hunt of York, later to be acquired by Camerons (Hartlepool).

Only licensed Brewster's could sell Beer, and the inspectors regularly visited the beerhouses. Once a year all publicans had to submit a quart and pint pots for examination and no 'ale' house could charge more than a penny a quart.

Scarborough was allowed only two vintners, and their licences were renewed annually. As far back as 1564, a Mr Oliver Digle was fined a hefty ten pounds for keeping a beerhouse without a bailiff's permit and for selling claret wine with honey.

In 1929, there were numerous complaints to D.O.R.A. (The Defence of the Realm Act) whereby a London representative was engaged to travel from London to stay in various hotels in Scarborough under the guise of a guest, to see if any of the numerous complaints were justified. The inspector stayed at the Grand Hotel and was horrified by his findings later declaring it 'one of the worst cases he had ever come across'. The hotel, which had recently changed hands, had a blatant and deliberate system of overcharging for almost all beverages. Whisky was under-measured and not the required 16 drachms. The charge was 2s instead of 8d. The hotel was taken to court, fined a hefty seventy-five pounds and severally reprimanded. The Prince of Wales hotel was also found to be overcharging for beer and spirits and charged five pounds.

Like today, many of the pubs in Scarborough have long since disappeared. In 1810, there was a pub called Five-Man Boat which was on East Sand Gate and owned by Mathew Watson, which we see from this advertisement was offered for sale in 1810.

SCARBOROUGH.

To be SOLD by AUCTION,
By Mr. JOHN KINGSTON,
On the Premises,

On Wednesday the 7th of March, 1810, at six o'clock in the evening,
Subject to such conditions as shall be then produced,

ALL that Valuable and Well-Accustomed PUBLIC-HOUSE, known by the name of the FIVE-MEN-BOAT; situate at the EAST-SAND GATE, SCARBOROUGH, and now in the occupation of Mr. Matthew Watson, the owner; containing four Rooms, with a good Kitchen, Brewhouse, Scullery, and Yard, on the ground floor; four Lodging-Rooms and a Dining-Room, on the second floor; four Garrets and a Gallery, on the third floor; also three good Cellars:—the whole being well calculated for carrying on an extensive business.

N. B. The premises are pleasantly situated, having a good sea prospect; and a Plat of Ground before the same, now used for laying Timber upon; which is very convenient for carrying on the Block-Making, or any other business connected with the Shipping interest: and are well supplied with hard and soft water.

. For particulars, apply to Mr. Matthew Watson, the owner.

Hull Packet March 1810

On Newborough, there were a few forgotten pubs, such as New Inn, Grey Horse, The London Inn – Pied Bull, Black Bull (later The Bull) – Balmoral Hotel and the Beverley Arms.

It was from The Beverley Arms that John and James Donkin, who were the father and brother of Blind Billy Donkin, a well-known figure in Scarborough who despite being blind walked around Scarborough selling pies, and he kept a plank of wood on the beach which he would place across the stream that ran from the sea under Cliff Bridge. The Beverley arms also ran a four-horse carriage twice a week from Scarborough-Hull. The family were fined a hefty twenty pounds back in 1811, for passing the Royal Mail carriage in Beverley and beating it into Hull. It seems 'speeding' fines are not such a new thing.

In 1869, James Bumby the landlord of The London Inn was arrested for the manslaughter of one of his customers, a Mr Thompson. Attached to the inn was a dram shop which opened directly onto Newborough. In April 1869, Mr Thompson was in an advanced state of intoxication, and he was loud and rowdy in the dram shop causing a nuisance to the other customers. The Landlord Mr Bumby lost his patience with this undesirable customer and grabbed him by the scruff of his neck and threw him to the street. Mr Thompson fell on his forehead with force and made no further sound. Alarmed, Mr Bumby checked to see if he was breathing and paid a member of the watching crowd a sovereign to take the man away. Police were called who assisted in carting the man to the Workhouse, where he died a few hours later. Mr Bumby was arrested and transported to York Jail to stand trial for manslaughter. The coroner then found that Thompson had died from a skull fracture, no doubt caused after his fall on the street.

At the trial, the jury was persuaded to accept a plea of not guilty and the lawsuit was dismissed. The Judge stopped the case, stating: 'The man was drunk, and he could not stand up properly! It would not do to turn a decent man into a criminal for life, just because of a drunken man who also had very unhealthy bones!' Mr Bumby was discharged and allowed to carry on running his pub.

The Elephant & Castle was situated on Cross Street in the centre of the 'market' and ideally placed for travellers. In 1832, a Mr Francis Johnstone found himself in the bankruptcy court after buying the freehold of this inn for seven hundred and fifteen pounds – a considerable sum back then. It seems that Mr Johnstone had borrowed the money from a Mr Duesberry; business had not gone as expected for Mr Johnstone who had closed the inn, and not paid Mr Duesberry back. Consequently, the inn was put up for sale and the advertisement described the business as being in a 'good condition, with a Brew- House yard attached to it and outbuildings, two stables for ten horses with a granary/hay chamber in a yard called Bird-Yard.'

The lease on the Elephant & Castle came for sale in 1884 and during the time up to 1894 had over seven tenants/licensees. In 1894, the Chief Constable of Police objected to the renewal of the pub's licence as the Landlord the previous year was convicted of allowing drunkenness on the premises, and that the pub was an inconvenience to the neighbourhood. The borough surveyor was called in; he certified that there were a further eight other ale houses within a radius of 100 yards.

In the landlord Mr Watson Harland's defence, a local police officer confirmed that the pub was now well-conducted and Mr Harland a credible character. The bench granted a licence and warned Mr Harland to be careful in future.

Scarborough's earliest licensed premises was the Three Mariners at 55 (now 65) Quay Street, which dates to 1300. The property is brick fronted and it is understood that there was a timber building next door which was once a part of the inn's structure together with a third building which were both demolished.

There was at one time a figure above the door recovered from the sea in 1874.

The inn was closed in 1913, and a year later Mr Burrows saved the property from demolition. Known locally as 'The Smugglers Den' it then ran as an antique show-house where people came from all over the country to view the various antiques such as nautical pieces of china, model boats and rich antique furniture. As the war approached the museum was closed and used for storage.

The old inn had four main rooms: two downstairs and two upstairs. Secret panelling was evident behind the beautifully carved interior panelling and fireplaces. A secret passage connected every room. Behind the panelling of one of the upstairs bedrooms could be found a smaller place, where it is reported that smugglers hid from the 'Press Gangs'. Near the first-floor landing was a small circular window which no doubt scrutinised many a caller before entry.

A rumour exists that this is the inn where Captain John Paul Jones drank his liquor and yarned.

The property is now a private house.

*

Scalby Mills

Scalby Mills, Scarborough

The area where Scalby Mills is situated is known as 'The Sea Cut' and previously the home of four mills, two of which are still in existence. Scalby High Mill, now High Hill Farm, which dates to 1609 a grade II listed building. The Corn Mill operated as Newby Bridge was opened in the mid-18th century and was closed by the 1950s. Another mill is now the Youth Hostel.

Scalby Mills (Public House) was originally a mill used for grinding corn. Before being transformed into a tearoom by Mrs Paranaby in 1858, the mill had many problems. In 1821, it suffered a severe fire. The property must have been repaired as it was offered for sale in 1834, by the assignees of miller, Mr Joseph Robinson. Further tragedy struck when in 1857 following Scarborough's most torrential floods the

265

property was entirely washed down by the strong current of water, so much so that the occupants seeing the water rising so rapidly were compelled to take their chances through the storm and head for a neighbouring farm for shelter. It was around this time that the mill became a tearoom, which was a success and soon after began the annual farmers' son's tea feast, an event that farmers' daughters also enjoyed.

By 1876, Scalby Mills and its surrounding area were owned by the Muston & Yeddingham drainage Company which included such eminent people as Sir George Cayley and the engineer William Chapman. This company's purpose was to drain the area and that of the mill dams. This company bought Scalby Mills and advertised for a tenant in the Leeds Intelligencer in 1879.

To Be Let by Tender for a fixed term of 7 years.

Scalby Low Inn Public House & Premises are adjoining.

The Premises are easily accessible from nearby Scarborough.

The Inn is well-known and much frequented. Money has recently been spent on refurbishment.

Lease available for signing at the New Inn Brompton 31/10/1879.

The meet. Author's own collection.

*

A Mr Cotsworth of York was strolling near boulder cliffs at Scalby Mills when he came across something protruding from the base of the cliff, on closer inspection he found it to be a circularly shaped axe 7 inches wide and 9 inches to the handle. This discovery was a weapon of proglacial origin belonging to primaeval man, and at that time (1906) the oldest axe ever discovered. The handle of the axe was itself a work of art and delicately carved in wood.

Perhaps not such a welcome discovery was again made at Scalby Mills when in 1927 a giant squid with tentacles 2ft long, and a 3ft body was found near the beach.

*

The fate of Scalby Mills changed again in 1921 when businessman Albert Corrigan developed a large holiday complex on the site. Formerly called 'Kingscliff Holiday Camp.' It boasted a range of activities such as slot machines, miniature railway and the ever-popular Astro-Slide. The development thought by man as a 'blot on the landscape' lasted 30 years.

Astro Slide. Photo credit permission Old Scarborough Photos. (Facebook)

*

Monkey Island

Monkey Island Photo Credit Old Scarborough Photos. (Facebook)

A favourite playground at Scalby Mills was a place called Monkey Island, a large mound of rock which projected out towards the sea known to the locals as an island, although not technically so. Why it was called Monkey Island is unsure, some say that it was due to a sailor who came to Scarborough with a monkey which escaped. There is another case of two marmosets – 5th Brazilian Monkeys – born in the area, the first known to be born in England, which could again be the reason for the name; still, folklore will no doubt continue for many years on the origin of the name.

Many an hour would be spent on Monkey Island, playing football or cricket, cowboys and Indians or 'I'm the king of the castle-you're a dirty rascal.' Not a care about what time tea was, no X-Box or Wi-Fi, just pure childhood fun.

The area was flattened due to erosion from the sea and became the home of Scarborough Sea Life centre, as it still is today.

Temperance Hotel

For those who wanted to avoid the demon drink, a temperance hotel was opened by Mr Thomas Whitaker (1813-99) in Newborough. Mr Whittaker had worked for many years in a cotton mill at Blackburn and became a victim of strong drink. In April 1835, he and his brother William signed the pledge and joined the newly formed teetotal society. Thomas Whitaker was elected to the Town Hall, a position he kept for twenty years. He also became Lord Mayor, became a Justice of the Peace and set up a newspaper 'The Scarborough Evening News', which was in direct competition to the Scarborough Post whose principal shareholder was George Sitwell.

Whittaker once printed a letter in the press suggesting that a recent tragedy of the deaths of twelve members of the Whitby Lifeboat crew had drowned because they were intoxicated. His words were not well received, and as a result, his effigy was placed on sticks and paraded around the streets of Scarborough smeared with red paint, then burned on the sands.

Thomas Whitaker died in 1899 an angry and disappointed man as no advance had been made to curb drinking. On the contrary, Scarborough then had 115 licensed beer and public houses in the town. Mr Whittaker is buried in Dean Road cemetery, and this is the inscription on his tombstone.

'Tell me not what story drink has been, nor what it is intended to be. I know what it is now. It is Britain's curse. It is the God of this nation.'

The Grand Hotel

The Grand Hotel in construction. Credit Kelvin Allen.

The Grand hotel must be one of (if not the) foremost of Europe's most architectural masterpieces. A work of wonder, which when seeing it every day it is easy to take for granted. Likewise, the Pavilion Hotel had its place in history as one of Scarborough's leading hotels until it was demolished in 1973 to make way for the concrete mess that replaced it.

Built on land formerly belonging to Mrs Cockroft, a boarding housekeeper who in 1862 sold 3 acres of land and her lodgings on the cliff to the Spa Cliff Hotel Company Limited for thirty thousand pounds to erect a large hotel. The plans for the hotel were ambitious, and the design very extravagant. Old houses including 'Wood's Lodgings' were demolished to pave the way for this new beginning, which would attract gentry from all over the country and make Scarborough the envy of all other towns. Local tradesmen had the opportunity of buying the salvage from the old properties.

Renowned architect Cuthbert Broderick designed the building. The Grand was the largest, the first purpose-built and at the time the most advanced hotel in Europe.

Many visitors to Scarborough, who do not know the story of the design of this unique hotel are not aware of its creative and ingenious design. The hotel is designed around the theme of time. At the time of building (alterations made since); the hotel had the following.

Four Towers to represent the four seasons. Twelve Floors to represent the months of the year.

Fifty-Two chimneys to represent the weeks of the year. Three hundred and sixty-five rooms to represent the days of the year. Furthermore, the hotel was built in the shape of a 'V' in honour of Queen Victoria. Such fabulous intuition went into the design of this prestigious individually designed building.

The brickwork alone consisted of six and a quarter million bricks which were made at Malton's brickworks (where Malvern Crescent now stands). The yellow bricks around the windows were from Hunmanby.

However, the initial plans were costly and over-ambitious, and financial problems soon followed, and by 1865 the Scarborough Cliff Hotel Company Limited had run out of money; thus, the company was dissolved, and all building work stopped. The hotel had already cost the company and its shareholders ninety thousand pounds (including the price of the land). There was too much speculation as to what would happen to the building, therefore the receivers put the property up for sale.

ALL that FREEHOLD PROPERTY and ESTATE of the above Company, situate on the East Side of St Nicholas Cliff, in Scarborough, with the Magnificent BUILDING intended for an Hotel, and other the ERECTIONS now standing thereon, the whole comprising an area of about Two Acres, and having a frontage towards the Sea of nearly 400 feet. And also the whole of the SCAFFOLDING, BUILD-ING PLANT, and MATERIALS on the above Premises, and in the Yards and Shops of the Company, situate in James's Street and Victoria Road, in Scarborough.

At the auction, a bid of forty-three thousand six hundred pounds from a gentleman from Leeds was accepted for a new company under the name 'The Grand Hotel Company Limited.' The chairman was Mr WM Firth. The building of the hotel recommenced under the supervision of Mr Archibald Neil of Bradford.

In preparation for the opening, the directors announced their joy of recruiting as manager Mr Augustus Fricour, who had previously worked in a similar position at the hotel Mirabeau in Paris.

The hotel opened in July 1867 to an inaugural banquet to an illustrious sprinkle of invited hierarchy and debutants from around the country.

The interior of the hotel was opulent with lavish and luxurious interior fittings, provided by Smee & Co of London which consisted of mainly white, Gris Perl and gold. The seating was in amber silk and brocade. The lighting was by four bronze gas statues; the chandeliers adorned with crystal pendants lit the room, there were thirty lounges and eleven miles of carpeting. A miniature railway ran through a tunnel underneath the building to carry laundry to the boiler house on the seafront below. The hotel had a hydraulic ascending room and probably boasted the first-ever lift in a hotel.

To stay at this exclusive hotel for a week would be three pounds six-shillings for full board, evening dinners were sixpence ahead. The management insisted on a dress code and strictly forbade the wearing of bonnets in the dining room, and all men must wear frock coats.

The German Bombardment 1914

Grand Hotel Restaurant after German Bombing in December 1914.
(Illustrated London News)

The dining room suffered damage when the Grand Hotel was one of the properties hit by the German's battlecruisers Derfflinger and Von der Tann accompanied by light cruiser Kolberg in December 1914.

A year later the hotel was sold to Scarborough Hotels limited and once again refurbished. It seems the company was not successful as in 1928 it was voted to offer the property for sale in the London Auctions, where it had a meagre bid of fifty thousand pounds. The auctioneers pointed out that the cost of the hotel should be in the region of two hundred and fifty thousand pounds as it had cost this amount to build and refurbish it, together with a further fifty thousand to equip it. The sale of the hotel was withdrawn.

The hotel owns three 'blue plaques' one of which is dedicated to Anne Bronte who made regular visits to 'Wood's Lodgings', demolished to make way for the hotel. Sir Winston Churchill stayed there during the Conservative party conference. In 1939, the hotel became the home to RAF trainees and the corner cupolas housed anti-aircraft guns. Furthermore, following the Iranian Embassy siege in 1980, the hotel was used in a covert training exercise by the SAS in preparation for other anticipated terrorist incidents. (Wikipedia)

In 1978, Butlins bought the Grade 11 listed hotel, the company better known for its holiday camps operated an inexpensive choice of accommodation. In November 2004, the hotel was purchased by Britannia from the Grand Leisure Group. It remains a popular tourist attraction and a major cultural part of Scarborough's rich history.

Ghost Stories

Some people have reported that they have witnessed ghostly goings-on in the Grand Hotel. Some of the activity reported over the years include guests witnessing items flying across rooms, objects falling from walls and doors shaking, and hearing screaming, singing, laughter and period music. Footsteps are frequently heard on empty corridors. A lady in a red dress is seen around the grand staircase and first floor. (Spirit Seekers, 2018) Perhaps the activity could be something to do with these poor unfortunate people. R.I.P.

1866

The building of the South Cliff/Grand Hotel was progressing well, a party of workmen working on the roof to the south seafront side of the building when one of the men Mr John Gratton, a labourer from Ireland, lost his footing and fell 70 ft headfirst onto Marine Promenade steps. The poor man died instantly.

1871

Reverend T Hall from Pontefract had come to Scarborough's Grand Hotel for a few days' rest. When he failed to come down for breakfast, the manager broke down his door to find the Reverend lying in a pool of blood from a gash to his throat; next to his body laid a razor. He had taken his own life.

1923

Lift attendant eighteen-year-old Mark Harrison had just taken the lift to the ground floor when the descending lift crashed down on his head killing him instantly.

1935

Mrs Mary Perry aged 49, a maid at the hotel, had gone up to her room on the 6th floor to have a cigarette. She must have fallen asleep and awoke to find herself on fire. She did not scream but dashed down the corridor into the staff room set aside for breaks and meals, by all accounts she collapsed into a wicker chair and died there.

When the discovery was made someone noticed a small portion of the woodwork on fire, then someone saw a heap of charred cloth and found that it was Mrs Perry whose body was unrecognisable. At an inquest the coroner ruled out that Mrs Perry had died because of fire started by a cigarette, he said that the cause was more likely to be an electric stove, as Mrs Perry had previously expressed her concerns about its safety to a friend claiming, 'one day it will burn me to death.' The coroner declared a verdict of Accidental Death and that 'it was mere conjecture how she came to be set on fire.' (Nottingham Evening Post, 21st February 1935)

The Pavilion Hotel

Credit Paul Thomas (Facebook)

Mr John Skelton Esq of Timperley was a businessman who owned a large house facing Alma Square and land opposite the Railway station. In 1869, Skelton arranged for builders to demolish the house, and he offered the land for sale as 'building lots with great taste'. The situation he declared was 'one of the best in Scarborough being near the Railway station, and having footage onto Westborough, and another onto Valley Bridge'.

Mr Skelton wanted to erect a first-class hotel on the site, which next to the Grand would be Scarborough's second purpose-built multi-storey hotel. He insisted that he wanted to create uniformity in the design and that the land would be an excellent situation for shops, with the remainder to be sold exclusively for residential or lodging houses.

The hotel was designed by the prominent architect William Baldwin Stewart in dark grey stone, with elegant central pillars. The hotel opened in 1870 and dominated Westborough and Valley Bridge Parade. (Northway did not exist then.)

Credit Allison Murray

Robert Laughton bought the hotel in 1908 and added a bowling green and a tennis court. The reputation for good food and dancing were excellent at the hotel, but residents of Pavilion Square were not happy with the constant excessive noise, not being able to park outside their houses, and guests piling luggage on the pavement; so much so they took the Laughton family to court. Mutual negotiation was agreed on the case.

The hotel was demolished in 1973, to make way for the concrete structure that replaced it. The houses in Pavilion Square still stand.

The Demolition of the Pavilion Hotel 1973. Credit Tony Amers.

Incidents – Jewel Thief

A daring robbery occurred at the hotel in 1872. A guest, Mrs Foster, was staying at the hotel, as was Mr Tomas Anderson, apparently a part of the 'swell mob' (organised London thieves). Mrs Foster had left her room to watch the launch of the town's new lifeboat when Anderson took his chance and locked himself inside Mrs Foster's room. On her return, Mrs Foster was shocked to find that she could not get into her room and went to complain to the manager. On her return, she passed Mr Anderson on the stairs and found her door open and all her jewellery valued at two-hundred pounds gone!

The hotel informed the police, and PC Sollitt rushed to the railway station armed with a description of the accused. He checked all the carriages, but the man was not there. Suddenly, a man following Anderson's description came running from the luggage room carrying a hatbox. He had noticed the police presence and opened the train door while it was moving to avoid capture.

PC Sollitt alerted the guard who telegraphed the York station. Anderson tried again to evade capture by trying to leave the train at York on the wrong side of the tracks. But it was to no avail as the thief was apprehended. The jewellery was all recovered from the hatbox he was carrying. He was taken back to Scarborough and put in jail. (Knaresborough Post April 23, 1870)

The Crown Hotel

The hotel opened to the public in 1845. Mr John F Sharpin announced in the press to all noblemen and gentry that the new hotel was ready for occupation, with one hundred and twenty rooms, hot and cold showers, and stabling for sixty horses and forty carriages. The only drawback to this elegant hotel was that it had no ballroom. The Crown proved so busy that an extension was needed. John Sharpin realised that having attracted fashionable visitors, it was up to him to provide a special room where they could entertain. He planned this addition; a dining room and ballroom was opened in 1847 and subsequently used by visitors for their private dances. Sharpin left The Crown in 1856, to run The Assembly Rooms and to expand his public career. An advertisement for let appeared in the press in 1856 and the lease was taken by a consortium of people known as Scarborough Crown Hotel (Limited) who took over control of the hotel.

TO HOTEL KEEPERS AND OTHERS.
SCARBOROUGH.
TO BE LET, for a Term of Years, and Entered upon on the 6th of April next,

ALL that Superior and Well-Established HOTEL, called the "CROWN HOTEL," situate on the Esplanade, in Scarborough, with the Billiard Room, Baths, Spacious Yard, Stables, and Coach-houses belonging thereto, and now in the Occupation of Mr. John F. Sharpin.

The unrivalled Situation and great capabilities of this Hotel are well known to a large class of Visitors frequenting the above celebrated watering place, and must always command a first-rate Business.

The House possesses a Frontage towards the Sea of 150 feet, and its interior arrangements are of superior order. It contains, in addition to an elegant and spacious Drawing Room, a large Dining Room, 16 or 20 private Sitting Rooms, and 120 Bed Rooms; excellent Cellarage, well adapted for an extensive Private Wine Trade, and every other requisite convenience.

Further Particulars may be obtained on application to ROBERT WILLIAMSON, Esq., Scarborough; or Messrs. HESP, UPPLEBY, & MOODY, Solicitors, Scarborough.

Scarborough, 17th September, 1856.

Yorkshire Gazette September 1856

The Royal Hotel

SCARBOROUGH HOTEL,
Boarding-House & Assembly-Rooms, near the Cliff.

MR. DONNER respectfully informs his Friends and the Public, that this House, which was so greatly enlarged Four Years ago, has recently undergone further Alteration and Improvement, and that it is now open for the Reception of Company for the Season. These well known Premises, commanding a fine View of the Sea, are furnished in a very superior Manner, and afford every Convenience and Accommodation, not only as a BOARDING-HOUSE, but for private Families and Parties. The Assembly-Rooms and Billiard-Rooms are attached to the House, and there is good Stabling, Carriage-Houses, Post-Chaise, and careful Drivers.

Mr Edward Donner purchased the Long Room towards the turn of the century, and these became popularly known as 'Donner's Rooms' to early 19th century visitors. As we see from the above-classified advertisement, Mr Donner extended the hotel in 1817. Edward Donner described himself as a 'Wine Merchant', but he was one of the first twelve (Scarborough Corporation) and soon after a senior bailiff.

The 'Long Room' was Scarborough's first hotel which had forty bedrooms all furnished in a superior manner, a ballroom, musicians' gallery, rooms for billiards and gaming. Scarborough Corporation gave a retirement dinner at Donner's Long Room in 1832 in honour of Charles Manners Sutton who had been an MP for Scarborough between the years 1806-1832. Manners was also the Speaker of the house of commons for eighteen years and Judge Advocate General. Presiding over this lavish dinner which included all fresh fayre and a selection of wines, champagne and the most excellent ports was Edward Donner and John Woodall.

*

After Donner's death, the hotel was put up for lease. In 1866 a Mr John Hall advertised in the Hull Packet (1866) that his lease on the Royal Hotel had come to an end and that the entire contents of the hotel were up for sale. This sale included three hundred walnut chairs, works of art, silver cutlery and ornaments, all the carpets and curtains, furniture and a cellar full of wines and spirits. The lease was taken again by a Mr William Jancowski who announced that he had extensively refurbished and completed extensive alterations to the hotel. Unfortunately, he did not have much time to see his efforts come to fruition as he died two years later.

In 1870, The Royal Hotel Company Scarborough Limited was formed to run the hotel, an advert was placed in the press for a manager and a chef. Shares were offered for sale in the company at ten pounds each. The company was wound-up in 1893 along with others in Scarborough, Filey and Ravenscar.

The Royal was one of the hotels damaged in the German bombardment in December 1914.

Nottingham Evening Post 17 December 1914

Britannia Hotels Limited bought the hotel in 2012 from English Rose Hotels after it had gone into administration.

Incidents – The Royal Hotel

An alarming rumour circulated in Scarborough in September 1881 that there had been a murder at the Royal Hotel. Unfortunately, this story proved to be true. The Royal has been one of the most aristocratic hotels in town holding an Assembly (Ball) each Friday evening.

Amongst the company were two young gentlemen Mr Joseph Norris of Taunton and Mr Meynell Collier from London.

The dance finished around 3 am when an intoxicated Mr Norris and the others retired to the smoke room. Soon after Norris could be heard loudly declaring that 'he did not think much of the ladies at the ball.' Collier responded saying he was a 'brainless idiot, and an unsophisticated outsider and a cad!' To these words, Norris arose from his chair and lit a cigarette. Norris continued using profanity towards Collier. Collier warned him that if he did not stop it, then he would knock him out! Unperturbed, Norris instantly repeated the profanities. Collier struck Norris twice in the face, on the second blow Norris reeled backwards and fell heavily. When Norris did not get up Collier, and a few others, went to his assistance and found him bleeding profusely from the nose and in a dazed, confused state. Medical assistance came and it soon became clear that the man was dead. Mr Pattison, the Chief Constable, was called for and upon hearing the facts took Collier into custody.

Collier did not resist arrest and simply said 'Yes, it's a bad job; I'm sorry.'

Further investigations revealed that both men were not previously acquainted and had a dispute over a certain young lady to whom both men were acquainted. Collier was charged with the manslaughter of Norris and remanded in custody.

There was an inquest at a crowded Scarborough Town Hall, and reports confirmed that Mr Collier was a well-respected man of independent means; bail was posted and paid at five hundred pounds, and Collier released on bail.

At the coroner's inquest, reports proved that Collier was wearing a large ring weighing eleven pennyweights on his finger, which most likely acted as the weapon in this incident.

However, the coroner's findings were that the deceased was in a bad state of health, the lungs, brain, and heart were all diseased, and that Norris could have died at any time due to large consumptions of alcohol. Collier was released, the jury finding that 'the deceased had given Collier provocation'.

*

Scarborough at War

The German raid on Scarborough December 1914

A t the start of the Great War in 1914, the Imperial German High Seas
Fleet launched a surprise attack on England's coast.

Without warning one December morning, the huge menacing
shapes of German battlecruisers emerged close to Scarborough, Whitby
and Hartlepool. At first, locals assumed they were Royal Navy ships, but
that all changed when the massive gun turrets turned towards the town,
firstly at the Castle then they opened fire on innocent people, killing
eighteen including a fourteen-month-old baby called John Shield Ryalls,
who lived at 22 Westbourne Park. The child died instantly as a shell tore
through his bedroom. A lady and her daughter were killed in the street.
A Miss Banks who lived on South Cliff witnessed the attack saying 'the
first shell came with a tremendous noise which shook the house like a
deck of cards, hundreds of shots fired in quick succession.' At first, she
thought it was coming from the Castle.

Shopkeeper, Mrs Emily Merryweather of Prospect Place was one of the victims; she opened the front door of her shop to let a couple of women into her house when she was struck, her body badly mutilated in the explosion. Another lady ran into one of the hotels to use the telephone and was struck and died instantly. Justice of the Peace, Mr John Hall was killed in his bedroom while dressing, minutes later his grandson was found dead. Witness, Annie Sagar states that the Bennet family at 2, Wykeham Street – two adults and two children – were all killed 'when a shell came flying past – it smashed a lot of windows in Gladstone Road School and went clean through Mrs Bennett's house,' she said. 'The place was blown up, and things went flying in all directions.' Ada Crow, 28, also died, sadly, her soldier fiancé arrived to visit her that evening, unaware of what had happened.

2, Wykeham Street, where Mrs Bennett and her two children perished.
(Hull Packet)

Witnesses reported that they saw many injured people carried through the streets on stretchers. Many people took refuge in the cellar of their houses. While others ran from their houses grabbing Christmas cakes as they went, (which were reportedly expensive then).

Almost every street in Scarborough was damaged to some degree, as was the Castle, hotels and churches, including All Saints and St Mary's. The gable end of the Town Hall blew away, and the sea-bathing infirmary severally damaged. Fortunately, the inhabitants, including some Belgium soldiers, all escaped. Shells played havoc with property along the foreshore. Luckily, as it was the winter season, the loss of life was not as great as it could have been if the raid had occurred in the height of the summer season.

Kaiser Wilhelm II had intended to intimidate England by launching these daring attacks, but he underestimated the wrath that this unprovoked attack had on the country – the nation was outraged. Winston Churchill labelled the Germans 'baby killers' and posters reminding people of the horrors of Scarborough's plight appeared all over the country in a patriotic surge to get men to enlist in the services and to fight for their country. The poster read 'The wholesale murder of innocent women and children demands vengeance. Men of England, the innocent victims of German brutality, call upon you to avenge them. Show German barbarians that Britain's shores cannot be bombarded with impunity.' A further campaign shortly afterwards urging people to go to their nearest recruiting station read 'Scarborough - up and at 'em' now.

WikiCommons

There were over 1,000 high explosive shells fired during the raids to Scarborough, Whitby, and Hartlepool. British public opinion was outraged and the cry of 'Remember Scarborough' was central to the military recruiting campaign that followed.

1918 saw Britain victorious in the war against Germany, but with the seeds of future conflict sown, and not long after the end of 'the war to end all wars', a second, even more destructive conflict started.

To pay respects to the brave men and women that sacrificed their lives for the freedom of others a seventy-five-foot war memorial was erected on the summit of Oliver's Mount. A commanding position and visible for miles around. The unveiling watched by fifteen thousand people, with twelve bronze tablets stating the names of the fallen.

*

The Second World War

Prime Minister Neville Chamberlain in response to the Munich Agreement declared that there would be 'Peace for our time' when as a precaution along with the rest of the country gasmasks were in the process of being distributed to Scarborough residents. Refugees arrived from all over the country, with a total of fourteen-thousand families billeted into Scarborough.

With the onset of the war Scarborough town was prohibited, the beach and the foreshore resembling more of a battlefield with barricades and barbed wire than its renowned reputation as 'England's first-holiday resort'. The armed forces requisitioned boarding houses and even the Spa. The refugee committee following some initial hostility agreed to accommodate eighty Basque children all boys between the ages of 12-15. They were located to Harwood Dale, Cloughton six miles from Scarborough. The committee was quick to point out that all the children were inoculated and would not come into Scarborough during the season.

In March 1941, ninety-eight German planes armed with high explosive bombs and mines flew over the villages of Folkton and Flixton, then subjected Scarborough to indiscriminate bombing known after that as the 'March blitz' causing loss of life and devastation. The printing firm of EWT Denis was badly damaged, luckily the nightshift had finished fifteen minutes earlier. In North Marine road an entire family lost their lives: mother, father and four children. A bomb exploded on Commercial Street, completely flattening a row of houses.

On May 8, 1945, Germany surrendered, and the war was over. Victory celebrations took place all around the country; Scarborough joined in the festivities with street parties. Hotels re-opened, and the lights switched back on at night. At last, holidaymakers began to return and after many years of rationing the town much like the rest of the country eventually returned to normal.

Victory celebration West Place Scarborough. Credit Yorkshire Post 1945

*

Part Four Shopping, Sport & Leisure

Dumple Street 1850s

The first recorded butcher's shop in Scarborough occurs from a deed in the Rievlaux Abbey (T. Pearson, 1994). There were various shops scattered around selling everything from ham to straw. Small streets such as Globe Street, Merchants Row and Dumple Street offered every ware one could want. Dumple Street (demolished 1930s and replaced by Friargate) had many shops from William Ellis and John Parkinson's Taylors shops to James Cass Butchers. There was also delightful hotcakes and bacon from Lizzie Richardson's.

Eastborough was created by the Corporation to provide a wider shopping area and a more direct route to the harbour rather than the narrow winding streets of Leading Post Street and Merchants Row. Until 1722 the only access to the beach was down Merchants Row and West Sandgate. At his expense businessman John Bland constructed Bland's Cliff giving much-needed access to the sands and the foreshore, hence the name.

Boyes Store. 'The Rem.'

In 1881, Mr W.M. Boyes opened his first shop at 12, Eastborough. Mr Boyes suffered a tragedy that same year when his seven-year-old son Thomas Allanson Boyes was run over by a horse and cart and its driver James Miller was imprisoned for manslaughter for killing the boy because of his furious and reckless driving.

Boyes store sold remnants at affordable prices, the shop was known affectionately as 'The Rem'. Scarborough was poor at the time, so housewives welcomed buying material cheaply to make their clothes and furnishings. Boyes soon needed more space and moved to the premises on the corner of Queen Street and Market Street previously the home of 'Hepworth's'. Boyes became so popular that the premises soon became too small and was extended. The shop included an incredible 'Oriental Bazaar' selling exotic furniture and lighting from the Continent, and a household goods department selling anything possible for the home.

The Rem Fire. Credit Sheffield Daily Telegraph 1/3/1915

In February 1915, one of the biggest fires Scarborough has ever seen tore through 'The Rem' and the adjoining Queen Street Wesleyan Chapel. Witnesses say they heard a large explosion around seven in the evening. The fire brigade arrived together with a contingent of soldiers stationed at Scarborough who helped with the blaze, and hundreds of spectators who came to witness the fire. The estimated cost of the damage was seventy-five thousand pounds. Fortunately, no one lost their lives, but one hundred people were out of work for a while. The store was rebuilt and enjoyed continued success and is still popular today.

*

Westborough

Westborough 1900. Author's own collection Eastborough, Westborough and Newborough were the hub of Scarborough's shopping centres, with many shops selling all commodities.

With the opening of the railway and the increased influx of visitors to the town, many shops moved to new sites on Westborough. William Rowntree's home furnishers became a department store with ten bays of windows which held two-hundred radiant lamps. The shop was popular with both customers and staff as the employees got to share in a profit share scheme.

The shop sold most things from silk handkerchiefs to untarnishable jewellery. You could even have it packaged and delivered for a small fee. After eighty years trading the shop closed its doors in 1990 to make way for The Brunswick Centre.

Another shop, known for its high-end luxury and elegance was Marshall & Snelgrove on St Nicholas Street. A concierge dressed in green livery would be at the door, and if he didn't think that you were the 'right' sort of customer, he would not let you in. There was a large clock in the hallway and a lift to all departments with a well-dressed patient attendant and a restaurant that served the perfect ice-cream sundaes. The shop closed in January 1973, and became Marshall House, and partially demolished due to it being structurally unsafe. There have been various pubs and cafés on the site since its closing.

*

Sport

Horse Racing & Scarborough Racecourse

Sport in Scarborough has for a long time been an integral part of the community. One of the oldest is horse racing, which dates to 1758 when races were held on Seamer Moor. These races were not always well-conducted as in 1778 a provision accompanied a gift of twenty- pounds with the instructions 'that the race should be in accordance with the advertisement'. Dissatisfaction with the management still prevailed, and a Mr John Halley Esq certified 'that the plate should run in the Royal manner and that there were no fraud or collusion at the entrance or the running'. In 1782, Scarborough Corporation would only pay half of their usual contribution due to the significant number of horses that did not run. In 1789, the last race took place on Seamer Moor, which had recently been purchased by the then Lord Londesborough (Joseph Dennison) who asked the corporation if the races were successful, and would it be worth his while to allow them to continue, as if not he wanted to plant the ground. The Corporation responded that the races were not profitable, and trees and a pathway would be more beneficial to the town. No races were to take place in Scarborough for another fifty years.

SCARBOROUGH RACES, 1762.
On MONDAY the 19th of JULY inft. will be RUN for, on Seamer Moor, near Scarborough.

THE LADIES PLATE of FIFTY POUNDS, in Specie, by any Horfe, &c. no more than five Years old, and that never won the Value of 50 l. (Matches excepted) carrying nine Stone, Bridle and Saddle included; the beft of three Four-mile Heats.

On TUESDAY the 20th, will be run for, on the fame Courfe, the Noblemen and Gentlemen's Subfcription of FIFTY POUNDS, in Specie, by any Horfe, &c. Aged, carrying nine Stone, fix Pounds; Six-year Olds, nine Stone; and Five-year Olds, eight Stone, four Pounds; Bridle and Saddle included; the beft of three Four-mile Heats.

On WEDNESDAY the 21ft. will be run for, on the fame Courfe, the Town's Plate of FIFTY POUNDS, in Specie, by any Horfe, &c. no more than four Years old, and that never won the Value of 50 l. (Matches excepted) carrying nine Stone, Bridle and Saddle included; the beft of Two mile Heats.

On FRIDAY the 23d, will be run for, on the fame Courfe, a Give and Take Plate of FIFTY POUNDS, in Specie, by any Horfe, &c. 14 Hands; aged to carry nine Stone, Bridle and Saddle included; allowing feven Pounds for every Year under; the beft of three Four mile Heats.

All the above Horfes, &c. to be fhewn and entered at the Coffee-houfe in Scarborough, on Friday the 16th of July inft. between the Hours of Two and Six o'Clock in the Afternoon.

Each Horfe, &c. that enters for any of the above Plates (except Subfcribers of Five Guineas or upwards) to pay One Guinea Entrance, Three Guineas towards the next Year's Diverfion, and Five Shillings to the Clerk of the Courfe.—All the above Plates to be run for in the Royal Manner. Certificates under the Hands of the Breeders, for all the above Plates, to be produced at the Time of Entrance.—Three reputed running Horfes to enter and ftart, for each of the above Plates, or no Race: And if no more than one Horfe, &c. enters, the fame to be paid Ten Guineas, and the Entrance money returned: And if two enter, to have Five Guineas each, and their Entrance money returned. The Entrance money, each Day, to go to the fecond beft Horfe.

In Cafe any Difputes fhall arife concerning any of the above Plates, the fame to be determined by a Majority of the Founders then prefent. To ftart each Day at Four o'Clock.

N.B. Any Horfe, &c. qualified as above, may enter (for any of the above Plates) at the Poft, paying double Entrance.

For a short while, races were held on the beach throughout the season until a purpose-built racecourse built on the part of Lord Londesborough's Seamer Estate. The racecourse closed in 1898, following a meeting at the Talbot Inn where the directors chose to wind up the company. The course sold in 1920. Briefly, races started again in 1924 but soon ended.

*

Cricket & Football

Before the formation of Scarborough cricket club, people played cricket in the castle yard where according to Baker's the History of Scarborough (1880) 'many a player pursuing his ball would lose his balance and fall over the cliff'. This event attracted up to two thousand people, generally wealthy and ardent followers of the sport.

TURF ADVERTISEMENTS.

GRAND CRICKET MATCH ON THE CASTLE HILL, SCARBOROUGH.

THE ALL ENGLAND ELEVEN v. TWENTY-TWO OF SCARBRO', VISITORS, & DISTRICT.

THE above GRAND MATCH will be played on MONDAY, TUESDAY, & WEDNESDAY, August 24th, 25th, and 26th, 1863.

The following are the Eleven celebrated All England Players:—

G. Anderson,	G. Tarrant,
F. H. Paget, Esq.,	O. Parr,
A. Clarke,	J. Cæsar,
T. Hayward,	H. Stephenson,
J. Jackson,	R. C. Tinley,

E. Stephenson.

REFRESHMENTS supplied by Mr. J. Young, ALBERT HOTEL, North Marine Road.

The admired Band of the Scarborough (6th North York) Rifle Volunteers, will attend each day.

Admission to the Castle Yard ONE SHILLING each day.

NO DOGS ADMITTED.

J. MACKERETH, Hon. Sec.

Yorkshire Post Leeds Intelligencer 1863

At a meeting in 1849 at the Queens Hotel (later The Cricketers) Scarborough cricket club was formed, known initially as 'The Queen's Club'. Sir Harcourt Johnstone Bart Esq, (later Lord Derwent) and an MP for Scarborough became the first president, followed in 1876, by WE

Woodall. The club prospered under Woodall's guidance, and soon they could afford to purchase the freehold of the ground at North Marine Road at an overall cost of seven thousand pounds. To offset some of these costs the company sold some land, later used for housing. The ground was enlarged and levelled during the winter of 1871-1872 and since that time has staged local, county, and international cricket.

Scarborough Cricket Festival

The King of Games in the Queen of Watering Places

Without the input of Lord Londesborough (William Dennison), the Scarborough Cricket Carnival (as it was then known) would not have been possible. For many years he brought together Gentlemen players, and at his own expense, he entertained them. Those he was unable to accommodate at Londesborough Lodge he provided for in hotels and even went as far as keeping a house in The Crescent especially for the use of Cricketers. (Scarborough News, 1893)

Started in 1876, and by accounts quite a lavish affair, Lord Londesborough had two marquees for his guests and a separate marquee with the finest cuisine. Henry Walker Esq also had a marquee, as did the club's president Mr Hebden.

GREAT CRICKET CARNIVAL AT
SCARBOROUGH
Aug. 28 and 29, COLTS OF YORKSHIRE v. HAMPSHIRE.
Aug. 30 and 31, NEW FOREST RANGERS v. SCARBOROUGH
CLUB.
Sept. 1 and 2, SCARBOROUGH CLUB v. SCARBOROUGH
VISITORS.
Terminating on Monday, Tuesday, and Wednesday, September
4th, 5th, and 6th, with the GRAND COUNTY MATCH, MARY-
LEBONE CLUB AND GROUND v YORKSHIRE (return).

Yorkshire Post and Leeds Intelligencer 17th August 1876

Except for the war years, this annual sporting event is continual and is one of the most historic and importing events in the sporting calendar. Scarborough has attracted people from all over the world to watch first-class cricket. It has also been the host to many a great cricketer including WG Grace, Don Bradman, and Wilfred Rhodes who played his last game at Scarborough before he retired. Wilfred Rhodes died in 1973 at the age of 95, as a mark of respect Scarborough Cricket Club flew their flag at half-mast to commemorate this great cricketer and regular visitor to the festival.

Mr Levenson Gower and Lord Hawke were towers of strength for the festival, so much so that in 1930, in recognition for their valuable services to the club, they were granted the honour of 'the freedom of Scarborough'.

Mr HDG Levenson Gower & Lord Hawke 1930. (Leeds Mercury)

Lord Hawke had spent twenty-eight years as Captain of the under elevens. He became president of Scarborough Cricket Club in 1928 when he succeeded Sir William Middlebrook. He had a long association with the club and had made his first appearance at the festival of 1881. His playing connection extended well over a quarter of a century a feat recognised in 1906.

*

Football

In 1879, Lord Londesborough together with other members of Scarborough Cricket Club and with the power of electric light set up a football club at Scarborough. A football association member, and one of the oldest clubs in England until sadly, the club was wound up in 2007 due to financial problems. Initially, football was played at the cricket ground on North Marine Road.

The club was not compatible to play on the same ground as Cricket, so future football matches were played nearby on the recreation ground. During the early 1880s, the club participated in the Scarborough & East Riding County Cup but took no part in any league. (Adamson) Scarborough was invited to become one of the founding members of the Cleveland Amateur League, but they left after one season because as soon as a visiting club was beaten at the Recreation Ground, they would complain to get the result overturned due to the pitch size, which was too narrow. The club was also amongst the first to compete in the FA Amateur Cup. In the 1898–99 season Scarborough took a step up, by joining the Northern League Second Division. (Wikipedia)

FOOTBALL.

LORD LONDESBOROUGH'S FOOTBALL MATCHES, BY ELECTRIC LIGHT, AT SCARBOROUGH :—
THURSDAY EVENING NEXT, October 2nd,
SCARBOROUGH v. YORK.
FRIDAY EVENING NEXT, October 3rd,
SCARBOROUGH v. HULL.
Play commences at 7.30 p.m.
ADMISSION :— Upper Ground, 1s. ; Lower Ground, 6d.

York Herald 29ᵗʰ September 1879.

An interesting case was brought before Scarborough County Court in 1886 when the club's secretary Francis Pickup sued Middleton on the Wolds FC for damages of four pounds, nine shillings and sixpence for non-fulfilment of a football fixture. Scarborough claimed that the match should have taken place on the 19th December 1886, but instead, the Middleton team had sent a letter saying 'can you cancel our match as the players think you are too strong for us! If so, we will allow you 10 shillings.'

The Scarborough secretary did not agree with either the amount offered in compensation or the cancelling of the match and told the Middleton team so.

Middleton again responded, 'we cannot possibly get a team together to come to Scarborough. I have tried, and I have failed.'

As warned, Scarborough issued an invoice to Middleton for four pounds three shillings and sixpence, as that is the amount it had cost the club to send a team to Middleton. They also warned Middleton that if they did not pay, then they would report them to not only the Association but would sue. Unperturbed, Middleton responded saying 'of course you know you cannot recover this amount, the only thing you can do is report us to the Association, and I will try to bring a team over before the end of the season.'

No payment was received, so the matter went to court.

At the hearing, Middleton's defence claimed 'your boots frightened ours so much so that they dared not come back to Scarborough. Your boots were too thick, and our lad's shins are too thin!'

The judge, on hearing this most unusual case gave the verdict 'that I must give a verdict to the defendants. The agreement was not a money-making one. It was merely a contract for athletics formed for pleasure, morally Middleton ought to have fulfilled their engagement. Scarborough had to pay Middleton's costs.

Another incident occurred when rival team Whitby played at the Recreation ground in 1890. Whitby as the away team was guaranteed five pounds for their journey. A crowd of 1500 attended the match, and the topic of conversation leading up to the game was threats of what would befall the Whitby men if they won.

The referee was Mr W Sanderson of Olivers Mount School, and the Scarborough team included, Murray (goal) Hammer & Carlisle (backs) Beal, Barnes & Williamson, Richardson, Kidd, Tate, and Newton. Umpire Mr JT Bennison.

A fast and exciting game with Scarborough leading 1-0. Scarborough scored the second goal in the second half, to which the Whitby goalkeeper declared had not gone under the bar. The referee disagreed, and the goal allowed. Outraged the Whitby team walked off the pitch. The Scarborough supporters were incensed and demanded that the away team played the rest of the game. The Scarborough club said they would not pay Whitby the agreed five-pound fee unless they did. Nine players came back on the field and the game concluded with Scarborough winning 3-1.

The crowd were still not happy and 'mobbed' the away team as they tried to leave. Whitby centre-forward Drabble received the brunt of their wrath receiving a nasty blow in the mouth and was struck with sticks and umbrellas and kicked on the legs. Police were called and intervened preventing any further incidents. Still, a large crowd followed the away team to the train station hurling abuse at them all the way.

A statement followed by the Whitby Team who said they were justified in walking off the pitch as they did not think that the allowed goal was legitimate. They would not be coming back to play again at Scarborough.

A statement printed in the Whitby Gazette following the incident said.

'If football matches are doomed to degenerate into such wretched scenes as this one detailed here 'the sooner they cease, the better.' (Whitby Gazette, 17th January 1890.)

*

In 1898, Scarborough Corporation offered the club a 14-year lease on four and a half acres of land at Seamer Road at an annual rent of twenty-five pounds a year. The club was responsible for levelling the ground. The club was then known as Scarborough Athletic. The club began to develop, with more success in local Scarborough & East Riding County Cup competitions and the creation of a reserves team who would play in the newly created Scarborough League.

The Second Division of the Northern League was abolished in 1900; this saw Scarborough and two other clubs admitted to the single Northern League division. Around this era the league was strong. It was during the early 1900s that Ocky Johnson debuted, the most prolific goal scorer in the history of the club with at least 245 goals, he was one of Scarborough's all-time heroes.

In 1906, Thomas Cole became chairman of the club and sought efforts to battle the club's debts; he would remain chairman until the mid-1920s. Scarborough won their first North Riding Senior Cup final in 1909, a competition which they would win many times; during the league in the early 1900s, they were consistently mid-table finishers. Scarborough joined a new league in 1910–11 in the form of the Yorkshire Combination, a mixture of professional and amateur clubs from the county. Scarborough managed decent results in the league, but after four years it collapsed due to lack of support from major clubs, leading Scarborough to return to the Northern League.

The First World War interrupted any meaningful sporting activities; many players including Tommy Renwick and Sam Horsman died during it. Scarborough was more fortunate than many clubs who were dissolved during this period, managing to survive through these terrible years. (Wikipedia)

Under the guidance of new chairman W.T. Medd, the club adopted professionalism in 1926, joining the Yorkshire Football League, with their first-ever professional match against Bridlington Town which they won 3–1.

The club suffered a setback in 1927 when a serious fire believed to have been started by children who were seen playing near the stand. Fortunately, the club was insured and soon repaired.

The club received sponsorship from McCain's, and the club changed its name to the McCain Stadium in August 1988. Financial predicaments have also been a recurring theme of the club's existence, and despite buying the ground from the council, the club sold it back in 1931, due to mounting debts. The ground was bought back in 1960. (BBC York)

Scarborough made history when they became the first-ever club to win automatic promotion to the Football League in 1987, thus ending – for a while – their non-league status, which had its fair share of ups and downs.

Sadly, the club's affairs did not improve, and the club after 128 years went out of business in June 2007. Such a great loss for football and the town of Scarborough itself.

*

Olivers Mount Motor Races

At the end of World War II, Scarborough Corporation wanted to do something to welcome the troops home, so it was decided that motorcycle races would be an ideal pastime.

The first race took place on Sunday 15th September with 350cc races taking place on Tuesday 17th September and 500cc races on Thursday 19th September. The first races were won by Denis Parkinson, Peter Goodman and Sid Barnett, with twelve-thousand people attending.

The layout has remained almost the same since those early days, the introduction of the Farm Bends section in 1991 (done to reduce speeds through the start and finish) the only alteration.

The circuit itself is 2.43 miles (3.91 km) in length and is not much more than a service road around Olivers Mount. However, the technical, narrow and twisty track requires a great deal of skill and bravery to tackle. Lined with trees and fences the course is a mix of fast, twisty straights and slow hairpin bends with the famous jumps section a highlight for many. And 70 years after the first-ever meeting was staged, it's still going strong. (Devitt)

*

Murders, Accidents & Misdemeanors

Over the years, Scarborough and its surrounding villages have had their share of murders and tragedies. Although rare when it happens, the devastation affects the whole community. Here are a few examples.

1768

John Smith an exile officer working in Scarborough had caught men smuggling in Scarborough and had seized several goods from twenty-four-year-old Mr Valentine Bailey and Mr Joseph Haines. A scuffle soon broke out, and the men assaulted Mr Smith. Valentine Bailey took a pistol from his pocket and shot the officer, killing him on the spot. The police came, and the men were committed to York Castle. Bailey was found guilty of the officer's murder. When hearing the sentence, Bailey was enraged and knocked a female witness down to the ground – the same woman who had entered most of the evidence against him. Before his execution at Tyburn (York), Bailey did eventually acknowledge the justice of his sentence.

1804

Sixteen-year-old Lydia (Ellen) Bell was staying at no 14 St. Nicholas Street. The former mansion of the Bell family. The head of the family Joseph Bell was a confectioner originally from York, who had a shop in Scarborough. The mansion, built about the middle of the 18th century, is three storeys high, and the street front is flanked by two fluted Ionic pilasters rising the full height of the building and supporting a stone entablature with an attic storey above. The date was 11th May, and in the mid-afternoon, Lydia was seen talking to a Private from the York Volunteers (stationed in the town at the time.) The young man pressed Lydia to take a walk out with him in the evening.

Lydia's father was very much against the friendship declaring his daughter too young to be forming such relations. A defiant Lydia disobeyed her father's orders, and at nine in the evening she left her father's house not saying a word to anyone. She left quietly by the back door, and through a neighbour's house. The neighbour saw her and tried to no avail to stop her by telling her that the man she pretended to be in love with had tricked her and that he was a married man. Lydia did not believe her and ran off to meet her love.

Lydia was soon missed, and her family frantically searched the streets of Scarborough for her. At eleven o'clock in the morning, reports came in that a female had been found dead on Cayton Sands. Poor Lydia's head was facing the sea, and her body revealed that an attempt had been made on her chastity, and there were many bruises on her body, particularly on her left temple, and her nose and eyes were greatly swollen. Her fingernails and clothes were ripped and torn implying that Lydia had put up a brave fight against her attacker.

There were feet marks found around the cliffs at White Nabb. A coroner's report confirmed that Lydia was strangled and that her attacker must not have been a resident of Scarborough and was ignorant of the tides as no doubt the killer would have expected the tides to wash the body away, but the sea had only wet her clothes. The coroner recorded a verdict of willful murder, and a hunt was on to find Lydia's killer.

This period was the height of the Napoleonic War. The York Volunteers were quartered at Malton having left Scarborough Castle, and an officer was arrested and examined by Scarborough Magistrates. Lydia's brother and her sister both said they had seen Lydia talking to the arrested man and that he had recently conversed with their sister at their father's door.

The prisoner denied this and declared that he had never at any time had any acquaintance with this girl and that he had only spoken to her once! On this evidence, the prisoner was discharged.

Four people swore on oath that they had seen Lydia with this officer before her death namely, Val Nicholson William Short, Robert Johnson, and Jonathan Simpson. All these four people perjured themselves to protect one of their own. According to historian Barker, all these four witnesses met untimely deaths. Val Nicholson is said throughout his life to have been many a time in a state of delirium, and while 'raving' said, he saw a woman coming towards him and called upon his wife to look at her and take her away. On his death-bed Nicholson admitted to murdering Lydia and that he had passed the blame onto the officer, that he was jealous, and the murder was a crime of passion. (Ann Register, vol 46, p.385)

Lydia left a ghostly legacy, and people say that her spirit haunts the house where she lived on St Nicholas Street; people have reported sightings of a young girl wearing a pink crinoline dress. While others say that the ghost of Lydia haunts the shore at Cayton Bay.

Here is a poem which was written for Lydia (Eleanor) bell from The Poetical Sketches of Scarborough. (Papworth, Wrangham, Combe) 1813.

Bellina's Ghost appears to rise,
Bellina, in her maiden bloom.
Sent, by a ruffian to her tomb,
Yon letter stone, she hovers nigh,
Swells, with her shriek, the seabirds cry;
And seem, in hollow tone to say-
"Thou soon shalt join my kindred clay."
Oh, I do to Bellina's door severe,
Be struck one chord-Be shed one tear.

*

The Murder of Mr James Law 1823

Mead's House, Burniston, February 1823 showing the window and position of the men when a shot was fired through the window. (York Herald 1823)

Visitors to Scarborough often commented on the low price of goods in the shops, especially tea, coffee, tobacco, gin, brandy and other spirits in comparison to other parts of the country.

To raise money to fund the fight against their enemies and the rebellious American Colonies the British government levied taxes on anything they could from windows to salt. The average pay was low with families struggling to make ends meet and pay for basic amenities, so smuggled goods were considered a necessity. Shopkeepers happily sold smuggled goods, and their customers were none the wiser.

Smuggling, on the coast, became a well-planned and carefully orchestrated operation often run by intelligent businessmen who covered their backs carefully with many planned escape routes and hiding places to store their contraband.

Smuggling usually occurred at night in bad weather when there was less chance of being caught. Marine Drive in the early 1800s was a rugged wasteland as was much of the coast with a maze of hiding places. Vessels were often black with black sails, which were difficult to see in the dark. Conspirators were on the shore shining a bright lantern to guide the vessels to a place of safety. Once on shore, a team would move the cargoes inland until it was safe to distribute.

The smugglers' biggest problem was avoiding the 'King's Men' (excise officers) who had the power to seize cargoes and impound boats and transport the guilty to Australia or hang them. The King's Men were a ramshackle set of people who often relied on informers or turncoats to prove their cases.

In 1823, a case of murder came before the courts. Smuggler, James Law of Staintondale, was shot. The perpetrator, William Mead, had fired a pistol through his bedroom window while Law and a couple of his friends were outside on their horses.

William Mead, himself an ex-smuggler, lived at Burniston, and for some reason, he had turned informer and reported on many of his old friends.

Mead's action stirred up much hostility and bad feeling in Scarborough and the villages. Farmers often gathered under the windows of his cottage, especially after Thursday market following a session in The Talbot where many jugs of ale were consumed. Once at Mead's house the 'smugglers would sing ironical songs mocking him. A song named 'The Pergerd Song' was a favourite.

The reason for this was that a few years before Mead shot Law. Mead had been found guilty of 'willful and corrupt perjury' in a trial Law took against him. Mead had testified on oath that he had seen Law and his son-in-law in a smuggling operation on Salt Pans (Cloughton) involving the smuggling of a cargo of gin, spirits and tobacco from a vessel from the continent. Because of the violent ferment which prevailed amongst the neighbourhood, the trial was moved to York.

The day before the shooting there was much bitterness and unrest in the town, and the Scarborough smugglers were looking for revenge. The target for this revenge was a woodman named James Dobson, who had given evidence against James Law on a previous case of smuggling. Dobson had gone to Mead's house to fetch a trunk and a box which he said he was repairing. On his way back to Scarborough he was approached by two men who got off their horses and took him, prisoner. When almost in Scarborough Dobson escaped and ran over the hills. The men chased after him and pelted him with stones and mud until Dobson was filthy and covered in dirt. The men who had by now been joined by a large angry crowd dragged Dobson all around Tanner Street kicking and beating him as they dragged along the road. He was severely beaten, breaking his ribs, rolled around in a dog kennel, then again paraded through the streets tied to a ladder. He would probably have died had he not been rescued by one of the town's officials. Here is Dobson's account of the events.

'A great many people dragged me along Tanner Street. My hat was cut off, my head, nose and eyes were dreadfully injured. I was very ill. My coat was torn off my body; the lower parts were torn. Mr Woodall rescued me and took me to Long-Room Street opposite the Town Hall. I had no feeling in my body. I then went to my house and was confined to my bed. I live opposite the Town Hall.'

A reward of one hundred pounds was offered for anyone giving information on the instigators of this assault.

CUSTOM HOUSE, LONDON.

10th March, 1823.

WHEREAS it has been represented to the Commissioners of His Majesty's Customs, that a violent Outrage was committed on the Person of WILLIAM DAWSON, of Scarborough, in the County of York, Farmer, on the 15th Ultimo, near High Peasholm, by a Number of Persons riotously assembled about him, some of whom seized him by the Collar, threw Dirt and Stones at him, kicked him over his Body, Legs, and Thighs, in a most inhuman Manner, and then dragged him into Tanner Street, in Scarborough, where they threw large Stones at him, which knocked him down, and by which, his Head, Nose, and right Eye were dreadfully injured, and the said William Dawson was placed in the most imminent Danger of his Life: The said Commissioners are hereby pleased, in Order to bring to justice the Persons who have been guilty of the said Outrage, to offer a Reward of

£100

To any Person or Persons who shall discover, or cause to be discovered, any one or more of the Persons who were actually concerned therein, to be paid upon Conviction, by the Cashier of His Majesty's Customs, at the Port of Scarborough.

By Order of the Commissioners,

C. DELAVAUD, Secretary.

On Thursday 13th February, Law and a couple of friends had been into Scarborough and had more than a few drinks in the Talbot, and on their return, home stopped outside Mead's House and sang the perjured song.

Mead had been expecting trouble, and he lost his temper, broke a window and fired his pistol directly at Law. Law did not die immediately, and knowing he was seriously injured went to his friend's house Dodsworth's Farm in Harwood Dale knowing that his injuries were serious he made a will. Law died seven days later. The coroner recorded a verdict of 'wilful murder' and Mead and a man called Robert Belt who was in Mead's house at the time was also arrested.

A crowd of fifteen hundred people attended Law's funeral at Scalby Parish Church.

The murder trial created much interest, the courthouse opened at eight in the morning, and the galleries quickly filled up with spectators anxious to witness the proceedings. Many well-dressed females were amongst them.

A girl from Burniston stated that she had warned Mead that Law and his followers were after his blood, this possibly swayed the jury whose verdict on Mead was guilty of manslaughter and not murder, and Bolt released without charge. Mead only served two years in York Castle, a lenient sentence for murder; perhaps he was more useful to the authorities as an informer? He later moved to Leeds and became a confidence trickster and was eventually caught and deported to Australia for theft.

*

The Death of a Child

The death of a child is a terrible thing, but when the perpetrator of the crime is its parent (s) or stepparent, the crime is so against human nature that it shocks the whole nation. Unfortunately, murders of this nature occurred in Scarborough in the 1880s and the early 1930s.

First, we look at the case of Alice Maud Pickering, a nineteen-year-old girl from Scarborough accused of murdering her son.

1880

In the summer of 1880, a man called Simpson was taking a walk-through Wilson's Wood when he saw something lying near the stream which ran through the valley. On approaching it, he regrettably found the body of a young boy about four years old. The body was in an advanced state of decomposition. Simpson alerted the police who took the boy's body to the 'dead house'. Immediately, foul play was suspected and the child's mother, a prostitute, was the prime suspect.

After making enquiries, Alice Pickering – known as Mary – was found in a public house in Leeds and arrested for the murder of her child, John William Pickering. She was escorted back to Scarborough.

Witnesses confirmed that they had seen the woman with a small child near Wilson's Wood. She was seen lifting the child over a stile. The witness was observing her through a telescope while he was at the cricket ground on North Marine Road. The woman, he said, was dressed in a black coat with a fur collar. The same coat Pickering had on when arrested in Leeds.

Another witness, a 'friend' of the accused who lived at 40 North Street, said that about eight o'clock in the evening Pickering had called at her house in a distressed state and said she was going to Leeds with a Mr Ted Myers. 'I asked where the child was. Pickering replied that she had left it at her husband's mother's house Mrs Allison.'

Following something she had heard this witness went to the mortuary where horrified she identified the dead boy as John William Pickering.

On the way back to Scarborough she changed her story saying that she hadn't left the boy with her mother-in-law but had given a boy a penny to take him to Mrs Allison's. Later, she made a full confession.

'My name is Alice Maud Pickering; I married Thomas Pickering in November 1877. We lived for twelve months at his mother's house on Seamer Moor. He did not treat me well! We went from his mothers to live at Ayton; he still treated me badly. I left him and went to live at Filey. He found me and took me back to his mother's house. We then went to live in Durham Street in Scarborough – a bad house. My husband made me prostitute myself, and he kept all the money! He went off with the landlady, Mrs Gamble, so I left him and went to work in service in Cayton. He came to find me and made a disturbance, so I had to go with him. We went to live in Burniston. Afterwards, I took a position with Mrs Woodall in Seamer Lane, he came and asked me to steal a sovereign. I refused then he said he would kill me. I left Scarborough and went to live in Stockton, but I returned to Scarborough and lived on North Street.

I took my child to lodge, and the rent was four shillings and sixpence a week, but I could not pay for it. I became acquainted with a man for the militia who treated my son and me well until his father put a stop to it saying, 'I was bad news'.

When in Leeds I wrote to my friend Miss Smith and asked her if she would take my son, she refused. I did not know what to do with him. I had no money and no home. So, I took him to the fields and left him thinking someone would find him and take him home, but I never put him in the water!'

Alice Maud Pickering was charged with murder and committed to York Castle.

The trial of murder was heard at Leeds Assizes on the 5th November 1880, before Justice Field. Mary Pickering (her preferred name) stated that she could not cope with the child, she had no means, no home, no money. She had tried to transfer custody to her friends, but they had their commitments and were not willing. Therefore, she took her four-year-old child on a dark wet, dreary night to woods on the outskirts of Scarborough, and the dead boy's body was found eight days later in a shallow stream which ran through the Plantation to the sea.

Mary declared she had not put her son in the water but had left him with pure desperation in the hope that someone would find him and care for him!

The prosecution argued that it was probable that by leaving the child that there would be the possibility that the child would meet his death and so she was guilty of murder.

The jury agreed, and Alice Maud Mary Pickering was found guilty of murder and sentenced to death.

Mary was taken to Armley Jail in Leeds to wait for the date of her hanging. However, a witness called Morley came forward. He stated that he could not read or write, but he, at the time the child was found, told Scarborough police that he had heard a child crying in the Plantation, the police had not written his statement down and had ignored him. He could not confirm that it was the same child as many small children walked through that area.

The public believed the sentence of murder was too harsh and that manslaughter more appropriate, therefore a petition containing almost fourteen-thousand signatures was sent to the Home Secretary asking that the death sentence be revoked, and that this woman had never inflicted any violence on the child, and that she had not drowned the boy, she had just deserted him!

The Home Secretary, the Right Honourable Sir William Vernon Harcourt agreed, and Mary's sentence was reduced to manslaughter and life in prison.

*

A Tragic Fire Queen Street 1898

The house and shop on Queen Street after the fire.

One of the saddest events ever to occur in Scarborough was a fire that took the lives of seven people. The tragedy happened during the early hours of 8th June 1898, when a fire destroyed a hairdressers/fancy goods shop in Queen Street, occupied by Mr and Mrs Brooks and their six children, Mary Ellen 12, Mildred 11, Darzell 8, Douglas 5, Elsie 3, and 18-month-old Ida. The father, Mr Joseph Brooks, escaped. But unfortunately, the rest of the family perished.

The following day the survivor, Mr Brooks, gave a statement detailing what happened that fateful evening. He said he went out to the pub around seven-thirty, he had two drinks in the Oxford Hotel and two in the Black Swan then he got fish and chips in St Thomas Street, then he went home. He was smoking a cigar when entering the shop, so he put it down on the glass counter (despite there being fireworks under the counter). He did not attempt to check on his children who slept in a back bedroom: two boys in one bed and three girls in another bed. His wife slept in another bedroom with the baby.

During the night, his wife Jane woke him saying she thought there were burglars in the house. Brooks told her not to talk nonsense, and he went back to sleep, soon after Jane Brooks saw smoke creeping under the door, she immediately went to the bedroom where the children were sleeping, the dense smoke overcame her, and the flames were too fierce. In the meantime, Mr Brooks said he tried to go downstairs to open the front door, but the smoke overcame him. Brooks then said that he broke a window in his bedroom with his hands and escaped through it. He said he called to his wife, but she didn't answer, he presumed she must have fallen and suffocated, so he climbed down the waterspout and managed to climb on the roof of the Queen's Head to safety. He then shouted 'Fire – someone quick bring a fire escape.'

The people of Scarborough were heartbroken that these young children and their mother had perished while their father had made no effort to rescue his family. Tempers were frayed. Stories emerged of how Brooks treated his wife and family and how abusive he was towards them, and allegedly he also had another lady friend in town.

A witness who had previously worked for the Brooks in the hairdressing shop confirmed that he had often seen Brooks strike his wife in the face and had seen him knock her from one side of the shop to the other. He also witnessed Mrs Brooks say to her husband 'You have threatened to kill me, why don't you do it now so that you can go off with your other woman!' The witness said he left the employment due to the constant quarrelling between the couple.

Furthermore, Brooks had recently insured the shop against fire for two hundred pounds and taken out insurance on his wife's life. He also had a stock of fireworks in the shop despite not having a licence to sell them. The shop was also up for sale for no less than one hundred and thirty pounds including the goodwill, actions that raised suspicions and fueled rumours. At the inquest, the coroner asked Brooks some direct questions.

'Why did you break the glass and not just open the window?'

Brooks replied, 'You cannot expect people to think of things like that at such a time!'

Coroner: 'Why did you not attempt to rescue your wife or children?'

Brooks did not answer and spent most of the inquest in tears, and completely broke down when the names of his six children were read out.

Coroner: 'As far as you know your children may not even have been in the house?'

Brooks again broke down. Outside the Town Hall where the hearing took place, thousands of angry people lined the streets. They were not happy. For his safety, Brooks was kept inside.

The funeral, conducted by the Bishop of Hull, was a sad affair. Two coffins contained the remains of the four youngest children. Mother and the two eldest children had separate coffins. The procession started from Elder Street where Mrs Brooks' mother and sister lived and travelled on route to the nearby cemetery. The road was lined with people on both sides of the road and along the way along blinds and curtains were closed to show respect.

Forty police officers were in attendance because of the hostility shown towards Mr Brooks. On the advice of the police, Joseph Brooks did not attend his family's funeral. If he did, he would jeopardise his own life and the peace of the town, instead, he was escorted to the train station and quietly left town.

The inquest into the fire lasted eight days, at the end the jurors recorded an open verdict, declaring that the family died of suffocation due to smoke from the fire. They could not determine the actual cause of the fire.

Joseph Brooks sat through the whole inquest with his head bowed. The jury reprimanded him and expressed their utter indignation on his character, and that he had made no attempt to save his family despite ample opportunities. The jury did not believe Brooks' account of the circumstances and felt his actions were despicable and that he was guilty of culpable negligence and his movements cowardly and the affair a matter for the Public Prosecutor to investigate.

R.I.P.

*

1933 The Murder of Dorothy Margaret Addinall

Roy Gregory. Yorkshire Evening Post, November 1933

In July 1933, police became aware that an eighteen-month-old baby girl was missing from her home in Scarborough – Dorothy Margaret Addinall, the illegitimate daughter of Mrs Gregory. Mrs Gregory, after the birth of her child, had married Roy Gregory, a twenty-eight-year-old bootmaker from Scarborough. He was not the child's biological father.

Roy and his wife and child lived at 40 Queen Street. Mrs Gregory had not been very well and was admitted to an institution. The care of her child was left with her husband and his sister Ada who helped when she could. One evening in March 1933 Ada had placed Dorothy in her cot and left her with her brother to look after, the child was never seen again.

On her return, Ada asked her brother where the baby was. He replied that she had gone away, that she was okay as he had given her to some retired people and that she would be under a better table than he could give her; she had gone to live at a farm in Snainton.

Three months went by, and people became suspicious, and the police were alerted. Neighbours said they had seen Gregory in the cellar of his house moving bricks and stones.

Suspicions aroused, police questioned Gregory, but he was uncooperative and refused to answer their questions. Three months after the child's disappearance he gave a statement saying that he had given the child to a Mr Smith of Henrietta Street in London. When the police asked who Mr Smith was and how did he know him, Gregory replied. 'I don't know, he's a commercial traveller from London, he sells labels, he came to my door. I wanted to get rid of the child, she caused trouble and is nothing but a mardy peevish child and the traveller said he would take her!'

By August 1833, the child was still missing. Gregory walked into Scarborough police station with a statement. 'I want to confess to what I have done.' He stated that one night while washing the child he became annoyed and frustrated and in a fit of anger he threw the child down hard on the bed, she hit her head on the wall and would not regain consciousness. He tried to rouse her, but she would not wake up. He realised she was dead and to clear himself he made up stories about her going away. 'I wrapped her body in a blanket and took her to Scalby Mills and put her in the sea.'

On 2nd August 1933, police excavated the cellar at 40 Queen Street and soon found a child's sock and bricklayers' hammer. Soon after they recovered the body of Dorothy Margaret Addinall in a three-foot-deep grave wrapped in rough sacking.

The child had seven fractures to her head. Roy Gregory was arrested for the willful murder of his stepdaughter and remanded in custody.

At the trial at York Assizes Gregory continued to plead not guilty stating that the child's death was an accident and that he had not meant to kill her, that he had tried to bring her round, but she was dead, so he had buried the body. The jury did not believe Gregory's plea, and on 21st November 1933, he was found guilty of the wilful murder of a child, sentenced to death and taken to Hull Jail. (Yorkshire Evening Post November 1933)

Gregory still defended his innocence and appealed saying he was misunderstood and that the murder was an accident. Lord Hewart dismissed the appeal. Gregory's lies had caught up with him, and on the third of January 1934, he was taken to the gallows at Hull Prison and executed by the hangman, Pierrepoint.

R.I.P. Dorothy.

Dear Readers

I sincerely hope you enjoyed reading this book as much as I enjoyed writing it. If you did, I would greatly appreciate a short review on your favourite book website. Reviews are crucial for any author, and even just a line or two can make a huge difference, it also helps to keep the history of Scarborough alive.

Thank you.

Bibliography

Adamson, Steve (1998). Scarborough Football Club: The Official History, 1879–1998. Yore. p. 8. ISBN 1-874427-92-5.

Baker, Joseph Brogden, 1882. The history of Scarborough, from the earliest date. With illustrations, maps, London

Birmingham Daily Gazette – Thursday 09 December 1954

Brodie A and Winter G, 2007, England's seaside resorts, English Heritage.

Buglass, J; Brigham, T (June 2008) "Rapid Coastal Zone Assessment Survey, Yorkshire & Lincolnshire: Whitby to Reighton" (PDF).

Historic England. Modern: Humber Archaeology. p. 57. Retrieved 26 October 2016.

Cole J, A sketch of the history of Scarborough, Cole, John.1824. Scarborough: John Cole.

Grosseteste. The Letters of Robert Grosseteste, Bishop of Lincoln, University of Toronto Press, 2010

Hinderwell. The history and antiquities of Scarborough and the vicinities. Hinderwell, Thomas. 1811. York

Illustrated Sporting and Dramatic News - Saturday 09 September 1876. Accessed 31/01/2018

Manchester Times – Saturday 09 December 1871. 'The cause of the illness of the Prince of Wales.'

Poetical Sketches of Scarborough [by J.B. Papworth, F. Wrangham, and W. Combe], illustrated by ... engravings ... from designs ... by J. Green, etched by T. Rowlandson GREEN, James., PAPWORTH, John Buonarotti., Rowlandson, Thomas., WRANGHAM, Francis., SCARBOROUGH, Yorkshire and COMBE, William.

1813. London

Rare Book Division, The New York Public Library. "Sea bathing" New York Public Library Digital Collections. Accessed June 30, 2018. http://digitalcollections.nypl.org/items/510d47dc-dca7-a3d9-e040-e00a18064a99

'Scarborough New Workhouse', Illustrated London News, 18 February 1860, p. 156

Theakston, S., Elsey, W. and Burton, R. (1859). Theakston's handbook for visitors in Scarborough; comprising a brief sketch of the antiquities and romantic scenery, &c., of the town and neighbourhood. Scarborough: S.W. Theakston, Gazette Office.

The Miriam and Ira D. Wallach Division of Art Prints and Photographs: Photography Collection, The New York Public Library. "Scarborough" New York Public Library Digital Collections. Accessed June 30, 2018. http://digitalcollections.nypl.org/items/c282d870-2289-0132-d549-58d385a7bbd0

The Miriam and Ira D. Wallach Division of Art Prints and Photographs: Photography Collection, The New York Public Library. "Views of Scotland and England" New York Public Library Digital Collections. Accessed June 30, 2018. http://digitalcollections.nypl.org/items/c352b310-2289-0132-2781-58d385a7bbd0

The Scotsman – Saturday 01 November 1845 Whitby Gazette – Friday 17 January 1890

Wills A and Phillips T, 2014, British seaside piers, English Heritage

Journals

REPORT OF The Lancet Sanitary Commission ON THE STATE OF LONDESBOROUGH LODGE & SANDRINGHAM, (1871). The Lancet, 98(2519), pp.828-831.

Websites

British History Online, Version 5.0. Accessed 28th May 2018. www.british-history.ac.uk.

BRITISH Newspaper Archives 1607-2013 | Newspaper Archive®

https://cayleyfamilyhistory.wordpress.com/history/settling-in-Yorkshire/Access 20/5/2018.

http://www.gravestonephotos.com/requestee/viewimages.php?scrwidth= Accessed 30/11/2017

https://en.wikipedia.org/wiki/Scarborough_Art_Gallery   Accessed 1/5/2018

https://sites.google.com/site/leedsandbradfordstudios/home/Oliver Sarony/Scarborough Studios/4/5/2018

http://www.bbc.co.uk/northyorkshire/content/articles/2005/09/16/s carborough_fc_history_feature.shtml/Accessed 31/5/2018.

Scarborough Maritime Heritage. Newspapers

British Newspaper Archive. (various publications) Herts Guardian, Grand Hotel, 8/12/1866.

Hull Advertisers Gazette, 'Scalby High Mill to Be Sold' 23/5/1834. Hull Packet, Scarborough Corporation 27/11/1833

Illustrated London News Historical Archive, 1842-2003 – Gale 2/10/1858

Ipswich Journal, Valentine Bailey, 27/8/1768.

Knaresborough Post, Pavilion Hotel, 23/4/1870

Leeds Intelligencer, 'Scalby Mills' 26/8/1879.

Manchester Courier, Lady Sitwell, 4/2/1899

Scarborough Mercury

Whitby Gazette, Robbery Grand Hotel, 25/1/1868.

Yorkshire Post

York Herald Stamford Mercury

Made in the USA
Coppell, TX
10 September 2020